WICCA FOR BEGINNERS

Collection of Essentials for the Solo Practitioner. Beginning Practical Magic, Faith, Spells, Magic, Shadow, and Witchcraft Rituals (2022 Guide for Newbies)

Tyne French

TABLE OF CONTENTS

INTRODUCTION

We congratulate you on purchasing Wicca For Beginners and appreciate your support.

There are numerous books on this subject available; once again, thank you for selecting this one! Every effort has been made to ensure that it is as informative as possible; please enjoy!

It's night, and the curtains of affluent homes are drawn tightly to keep out prying eyes. The living room is lit by candles. The smoke from the incense twists in spirals. Figures dressed in tunics sing in a language. Circulating water circulates around a rustic wood table. Sacred images above her, among the candles: A Goddess with a Crescent Moon on her brow; a God with a spear in his raised hand.

All movement is halted. A woman standing next to the Altar declares: In this sacred space and time, we now address the Ancestors: The Goddess of the Moon, the seas, and the rivers; The God of the radiated Sun, the valleys, and the forests: Approach us in this circle.

THIS IS THE PRACTISE OF WITCHCRAFT.

Two thousand miles away, a fifteen-year-old girl Affix a green candle to a photograph of a friend. She lights the candle in the Darkroom. After that, close your eyes. In her mind, she sees a brilliant lilac light enveloping this sacred space and time that we now refer to as the Ancestors. Ancestors: The Goddess of the Moon, the seas, and rivers; The God of the radiated sun, Sun, valleys, and forests: Approach us in this circle.

Upon seeing her boyfriend's broken arm, she sings a magical wax for healing.

This is also considered Witchcraft. These two instances exemplify Witchcraft.

Popular wizards are individuals who are dissatisfied with religious or physics-based beliefs; they have landed on the earth and its treasures. They looked within to discover the mystical powers of the human body brother and their connection to the Earth, and discovered that magic works.

CHAPTER 1:

BOYFRIEND'S BROKEN ARM, OF WICCA

The first signs of ancient Witchcraft / Religion date all the way back to 25,000 years BC. Dr. Margaret Murray conducted research and traced the ancient religion's origins. She perceived an unbroken chain stretching from that era to the present day of a religious system that spread throughout Eastern Europe many centuries before Christianity appeared. She presented evidence and hypotheses about the origins of this religion, which have garnered widespread respect to this day. Men and women relied on hunting for survival during the Paleolithic era. They would have food, skins to cover themselves, and bones to make weapons and tools only if the hunt was successful. Nature astounded them in such a way that they attributed controlling spirits to those forces, transforming them into deities. It is what we today refer to as "Animism."

As with every natural force, there was a god for hunting. Because the majority of animals hunted had horns, men gave the god of the hunt the appearance of a man with horns. It is here that magic meets this model of god worship for the first time.

The earliest manifestations of magic were sympathetic; they believed that if they moulded an image of a biscuit in the mud and then "killed," they would kill a real bison after hunting. Religious - magical rituals originated in this manner, with one of the men dressed in skins and horns, representing the god, directing the clay drum's "hunt." Today, caves still contain paintings from that era that depict this ritual. A goddess stood beside this god of hunting. This was not about hunting, but about fertility, because if there were animals to hunt, it was necessary for those same animals to reproduce in order to ensure their continued existence. It is unknown who emerged first, the god or the goddess, and it is irrelevant because there is no material to clarify this.

If the tribe was to survive, the fertility of its members was critical, even more so given the high level of morality prevalent in those days. For sympathetic magic, animal copulating figures are moulded in mud and accompanied in ritual by clan members. Numerous images of the Goddess have been discovered during excavations, demonstrating the importance they placed on the genital aspect of women, symbolising their fertility and sexuality. These have large breasts, a swollen stomach, and exaggerated sexual organs, but not the arms, legs, or face. With the development of agriculture, the need for hunting decreased, which resulted in the goddess's emergence.

She has now begun to look after the earth's fertility, as well as the tribe and its animals. Thus, the year was divided in half.

The Goddess ruled the summer, when food grew from the earth, while God ruled the winter, when food was obtained through hunting. Other deities (thunder, wind, rain, etc.) became secondary gods in the god and goddess incarnations. As man evolved, religion evolved into what it is today.

Men dispersed throughout Europe, bringing their gods with them. When new countries were formed, the gods acquired new names, though they remained the same gods. When man discovered how to store his crops in barns for the winter, hunting became even less necessary, and the God of the hunt evolved into the God of nature, death, and everything in between.

TIME FOR THE BURNING

It is referred to as a fiery era, one in which those who did not believe in or embrace the catholic religion were either burned alive or hanged (in some countries, it was illegal to burn anyone, so they were hung). It's worth noting that many of the people who died at this time were not witches, but rather people who were despised in their villages and thus accused of witchcraft. It's also fascinating to observe how Christianity's ignorance accused sorcerers of being devil worshipers and of murdering children, when in reality, such practises do not exist among witches, as we do not believe in the devil, as this contradicts the Goddess's burden and our love and respect for all living things. According to the Catholic Church, the total number of executions was estimated to be 3,000. Persecution was not uniform throughout Europe; it was initially concentrated in eastern France, Germany, and Switzerland. Numerous countries eliminated the practise of burning. The burning era and its persecution came to an end with the arrival of the Age of Enlightenment, when people began questioning long-held religious "truths."

This effectively ended the practise of executing sorcerers in Europe and America. More than the death toll, what matters to us about that time period is that the laws of inquisition were abolished. Today, we continue to face persecution because our beliefs differ from those of other religions, and while they do not burn us alive or send us to the gallows, it is something we must live with on a daily basis, especially those who live in countries with a strong Christian morality.

THE RESUME OF ANCIENT RELIGION

In 1951, England abolished the last laws against sorcerers.

Gerald Gardner published a book titled "Witchcraft Today" in 1954 in which he asserts that Murray's theories were correct and admits to being certain of it as a Warlock himself. He also argued that the Old Religion was on the verge of extinction, but to his surprise, as the book spread, he began to receive reports of Groups or Covens scattered throughout Europe. From its humble beginnings in Prehistory to the present day, the Old Religion has come a long way. It has grown tremendously and is now a worldwide religion, owing to all those who have chosen to embrace and publicise the faith in one way or another. To this, we must add that the Internet has introduced many more people to Wicca and piqued their interest in this philosophy of life, which, unlike other religions, encourages man to realise himself fully, freely, and thus happily.

HOW TO CONDUCT BUSINESS WITH PERSONS OF ANOTHER RELIGION

There is one thing we must always bear in mind: when we meet with people who do not share our beliefs, the term "Warlock" offends them because they immediately associate it with satanism. As a result, I always recommend the term "Wicca."

Apart from not understanding what it means, they are not as fearful. Another point to remember is that the burning era is over, and it has nothing to do with the animosity between Christianity and Wicca.

Everyone should follow their lead and devote time to studying their doctrines in order to remain steadfast in them throughout the moment. We must study and understand the basis for our beliefs so that when sharing with someone who does not understand, we are prepared to explain. What we believe and how we respond to your inquiries. Additionally, we must decide whether we will be witches "OUT OF THE CLOSET" or "IN THE CLOSET"... that is, whether we will declare our sorcery publicly or privately; either way is acceptable. It is our choice, and many times we must make the best decision for ourselves.

Today, many may accuse us of devil worship, of murdering men on "Halloween," or of gathering to invoke spirits. If we are aware of who we are and what we do, all of these charges will pass us by. Thus, the best preparation for dealing with adherents of other religions is to study; to be concerned about our beliefs, and to live accordingly. If we do, no one will be able to tell us anything, and even worse, they will resort to us when we have problems, as we will be the "NEIGHBORHOOD WISE".

Around 250 BC, the Roman advance compelled him to begin conquest of the region gala, which was occupied by the Celts, whose beliefs were greatly distorted, most notably by Catholicism, which adopted some elements, such as the organisation of his priestly class and the cult of Hesu, the son who made his own sacrifice to save men; the manuscripts or compilations of the studies of the disciples of the Priestly colleges were copied and secretly transmitted throughout Eastern and Central Europe. The Gauls had a highly symbolic cult; their doctrine believed in the immortality of the soul, and their cult was classified into categories similar to those of mediaeval monks; their priests were legislators, physicians, poets, and capable of communicating with the spiritual world; they attributed power to the stars and their influence on men and nature; they knew and dominated herbal medicine; and their priests were infallible fortune tellers, consulted by nobles and even Emperor Aure. In many cultures, they are also the final court of appeal, rented guns, for those seeking extraordinary assistance in obtaining a partner or exacting revenge on someone. The English term "witch" (sorcerer) derives from the Anglo-Saxon Wicca (with the feminine form wicce), a term that many sorcerers use today as a synonym for the "Ancient Religion." It is associated with the words "wit" and "wise" (wit and wise), as well as with a term meaning "folded," which continues with terms like "witch hazel."

The term "wicked" implies that in nineteenth-century England, the term "Witch" had primarily negative connotations. ("Warlock" (sorcerer), a term frequently used by later writers to refer to a male and lonely sorcerer, has a pejorative connotation in its original meaning; it refers to someone who alters or breaks an oath.) More neutral terms included "cunning man" and "cunning woman," which were used in the English Renaissance to refer to a town's seers and healers who practised what was referred to as "white magic." Other languages' words frequently convey the same mixed emotions.

11

WITH REGARDS TO WITCHCRAFT

Perhaps the most difficult is the Italian strega, derived from the Latin word for ulcer, which came to refer to a vampire. The Greek Pharmakos equates the sorcerer with the expert in poisons. However, the terms simply refer to the fact that a sorcerer is someone who practises some form of witchcraft. The French sorcerer, the German hexel and zauberin, the Spanish sorcerer, and the Russian vedyna lack the fear felt by the inhabitants of the Mediterranean towards the descendants of the dreaded Circe, who, according to Homer, converted Ulysses sailors into pigs.

While English, like Anglo-Saxon wicca, uses the term "witch" to refer to both men and women, the repeated English distinction between "witchcraft" and "sorcey" (sorcery) does not occur in many languages. The term "witchcraft" has almost always been used negatively, for historical reasons that reflect the prejudices of mediaeval clerics, who condemned anything associated with the world of magic as a sign that Christ had been replaced by the Devil. The twentieth-century wizards sought to rehabilitate the image of Wicca, or "the Art of the Wise," by admitting that mediaeval witchcraft was actually religious exercise. To my mind, this attempt to disentangle sorcery and witchcraft does little more than obscure the constant interaction between popular magic and more intellectual occult practises (so-called high or ceremonial magic). Contemporary witch meetings, for example, cannot be understood without reference to Renaissance ceremonial magic, which was revived in the nineteenth century by groups such as the Golden Dawn.

On the other hand, the ceremonial magic tradition, which we will discuss later, is replete with popular practises that reflect older perspectives. What do we truly know about the Western tradition of witchcraft? What I demonstrated was the existence of two distinct legends and a composite story based on facts. The first legend evolved over centuries of persecution, culminating in the nearly unbelievable barbarism of the sixteenth and seventeenth centuries. The second is the legend of the "Old Religion" of twentieth-century cult witches. The facts tell a complicated story of how popular magic in ancient Europe combined with the sunken wastes of Hellenic civilization to create the first legends, practises, and covert beliefs of today's hereditary sorcerers.

Given that I began working backwards, beginning with the second legend, in my quest to penetrate Tanya's magical world, this may be the best place for us to begin. We will trace the history of the "Ancient Religion," as told by nineteenth-century folklorists, and how it has influenced modern sorcerers. It's worth noting that Shakespeare's greatest works all contain the same ingredients that helped make La Semilla del Diablo a box office smash: sex, violence... and what's hidden. As with their contemporaries, Elizabethan auditoriums delighted in the presentation of ghosts (Hamlet), witches (Macbeth), and other supernatural beings (The dream of a summer night). After all, it was still a time when men and women could be held accountable for the harm caused by black magic practise. Over time, men like Scot and Hobbes' views became the norm for an urban, educated population. However, in rural areas, traditional beliefs - and associated fears - faded more gradually. Tanya recalls, for instance, that the residents of the lovely Devonshire region, where he attended school, accepted the presence of elementary spirits, fairies, in all things crescent. Such rural practises and beliefs are not unique to England, but are found throughout the Western hemisphere.

Primitive folklorists such as Jacobo Grimm made the connection between these schemes and the paganism that the church attempted to eradicate during the Middle Ages.

Witchcraft, in particular, was regarded as a relic of Europe's earliest religions, particularly the cult of Diana, the moon goddess.

13

At the turn of the nineteenth century, the American journalist Charles Godfrey Leland believed he had discovered conclusive evidence that the "Old Religion" had survived, even three centuries after his last appearances with news. He gathered a small but remarkable collection of material with the assistance of a young strega named Maddalena, which he titled Aradia or the Gospel of the Sorcerers. It contained a self-titled Vangelo or gospel narrating the birth of Aradia, the goddess of witchcraft, instructions for a ritual meal honouring Diana and Aradia, a collection of spells, and various legends attesting to the existence of Counter religion.

Aradia's references to oppression suggest the same turbulent period as the Franciscans and the heretical Waldensians (the Poor Men of Lyon), a 12th-century group that advocated a profound asceticism and great personal piety in opposition to wealth and style in the largely formal institutional church.

Through the mediaeval and modern ages, the Waldensian influence remained strong in northern Italy, and it is quite possible that this contributed to the general mood of the Leland manuscript. Apart from that, I have my doubts that the legend of Aradia was as ancient as Leland claimed. The entire nineteenth century was devoted to romantic reconstructions of ancient Greece and Rome, and the structural simplicity of the myth, in contrast to the convoluted versions of the majority of folk tales that have survived the centuries, suggests an intervention by someone familiar with the classics, with a gift for poetic expression, and with a fervent hatred for the church and landowner aristocracy. Leland expresses his conviction that witch covens (meeting rituals) are still celebrated within the Holy City. However, the spells and narratives he incorporates into his basic text suggest only the individualistic practises that characterise popular European magic in general.

Was there a gathering of sorcerers in northern Italy? In a region where witchcraft could be practised without fear of official repercussions, the absence of more explicit references to Group activities appears to be a sufficient indication that they did not occur. That nostalgia, which was prevalent among many of the period's occultists, explains why seemingly ordinary men dressed in exotic costumes, pronounced enchantments in an impossible language, and generally acted as if humanity's future depended on something other than the expansion of industrial civilization. However, the reality is that numerous groups dedicated to the study and practise of magic existed at the turn of the nineteenth century. Witchery, according to adherents of the Hermetic Order of the Golden Dawn in England and the Order of the Temple of the East in Germany, was a perverted form of Christianity, a worship of the Devil who did not deserve the consideration of educated men. The Aradla de Leland, first published in 1899, received little attention and was quickly forgotten. Margaret Murray, the woman who elevated witchcraft intellectually, is never mentioned in either of his two major works, and she is also not mentioned in Gerald B. Gardner's The Witchcraft Today, which initiated the contemporary round of revelations about the "Old Religion." According to Thomas C. Leffibridge, whose book Bruges reintroduced Leland's work to the modern public, "it appears strange and is likely to be drowned in some way for hidden interests." A more plausible explanation is that even the discovery of a sect dedicated to Diana in distant Italy will not demonstrate that the Middle Ages' witchcraft groups, if they existed, would have survived in the modern world. There is a two-century gap between Aradia and Margaret Murray's The Witchcraft Cult in Occidental Europe. Miss Murray did not pretend, in contrast to Leland, that organised witchcraft would have survived their persecutors. What he did offer was an extraordinary and profound study in support of his thesis that, while witchcraft existed, it was a distinct religion that coexisted with Christianity during the Middle Ages. This theory does not presuppose belief in miraculous facts. Despite the title of his book, Murray focused his

15

research primarily on the British Isles. It began with a critical distinction between "operational witchcraft," or the various forms of folk magic, and "ritual witchcraft," or the forms of a rooted religion at a pre-agricultural level of civilization. His theory is that this religion, which she claims has a god in the form of a man or a beast, well-defined rites, and an excellent organisation, survived the Christian church's advent.

The great witchcraft trials, which began in 1324 in Brittany with the prosecution of Alice Kyteler, were a determined and ultimately successful attempt by Christian clerics to suppress their former adversaries. However, as Miss Murray reconstructs, those prosecutions were not solely religious in nature, but also included a struggle for political power between peoples descended from Europe and its successors oriented by Rome.

What distinguished Margaret Murray's study from previous works on witchcraft was his complete acceptance of the material contained in sorcerers' "confessions." Their predecessors either took them at face value, as evidence of a perverted Christianity, or rejected them entirely as the product of the clergy's imagination. The Witchcraft Cult in Western Europe contains statements about what Murray referred to as the "Diánico cult." The sorcerers' devil - or god - was said to be a man dressed in black to conceal his true identity or covered in animal skin to represent the divinity of nature (the Cuckold God) that was the object of worship. The thirteen members of the group (twelve worshipers and one dressed as God) were destined to worship. Margaret Murray wrote The God of the Sorcerers ten years after her first book was published. By that time, I had fully accepted the notion that the Fairies of legend were the Pygmy indigenous peoples of Western Europe.

They were also the inheritors of the "Old Religion," and conquerors learned to adopt their customs in order to ensure their loyalty. As a result, they were adept at propagating the Diánico cult

16

among the most influential members of England's and France's royal courts. Murray had already advanced his thesis that Joan of Arc and the remarkable Gillesde Rais, who was assassinated in 1440 by a mass murderer, were both heads of sorcerer associations. In a second book, he included William Rufus, the English king assassinated in the New Forest in 1100, and Thomas Becket as adherents of the "Old Religion." He was referring to the four human sacrifices required at the conclusion of each seven-year cycle of a king's reign.

According to this theory, William Rufus died alone, but the other three were ritual substitutes, two of whom were canonised by the church they opposed. Instead of Carlos VIII and Becket, Juana and Gilles de Rais died. He was assassinated by Henry II. This extraordinary statement implied that not only the kings of France and England but also prominent members of the Catholic hierarchy, including the saint Archbishop Thomas Becket, were only nominal Christians. Additionally, it meant that the concept of a divine victim was central to understanding mediaeval politics. As might be expected, this theory resulted in Margaret Murray losing a significant portion of her reputation as a serious historian. Undaunted, she published in 1954, the year of Gerald B. Gardner's The Witchcraft Today, The Divine King in England, an affirmation of his conviction that British royalty had accepted the "Old Religion" from Roman to seventeenth-century times.

Margaret Murray's books have developed a following among contemporary sorcerers such as the Aradia de Leland. Above all, they established the legend of the "Old Religion," which has been perpetuated by Gerald Gardner, Sybil Leek, Alex Sanders, Raymond Buckland, and a host of others claiming to be current worshipers of the Cuckold God and the moon goddess. Nothing is known about the extent to which Miss Murray influenced not only the legitimization of post-1945 associations of groups but also their feasibility. There is no conclusive evidence that such associations existed in England prior to the publication of The Cult of Witchcraft in Western Europe in 1921.

At the turn of the eighteenth century, English law reversed its position throughout its history, in response to the tragic experiences of the Salem colonial magistrates and the new climate of rationalism. Individuals would no longer be prosecuted for witchcraft. Now, those are precisely the outlaw claims. However, this new law did not take effect until 1951, largely due to spiritualist lobbying and not because no one believed in sorcerers practising freely their knowledge without fear of punishment. However, in 1954, Gerald B. Gardner, a former plantation owner and customs officer in Malaysia who had retired to England's New Forest, published The Witchcraft Today as an affirmation that ritual meetings of sorcerers existed and that the time had come to make details of that science public.

He repeated the story of the "Little Town" from The God of Sorcerers in his book, for which Margaret Murray wrote an introduction.

Gardner believes that the Neolithic cult schemes, specifically the cult of God Cuckold, came under the influence of the cult of the Great Mother during the migration of a Celtic population to Western Europe's aboriginal pygmies. Until the Middle Ages, that Druid cult tended to adopt the colours of successive waves of invaders.

Contrary to Margaret Murray's theory, the majority of Warlocks considered themselves to be devout Christians. However, the Knowledge had endured, even during times of persecution. Gardner's preface to Knowledge is an enthralling tale. Gardner discovered that several of his neighbours in the New Forest region were members of a secret society founded by the theosophist

Annie Besant's daughter. It was the Congregation of Crotone, named after Pythagoras' esoteric group in former Italy. Several congregation members eventually confessed to Gardner, who had made contact with the last members of an ancient ritual group.

Meanwhile, Gardner met the elderly woman who led the group and was initiated into witchcraft by her. Gardner wrote a novel, The Help of High Magic, following the woman's death, in which he revealed the unbroken existence of the tradition of ritual associations. That was in 1949, two years before witchcraft was declared illegal in the United States. In 1954, he published The Witchcraft Today, lifting the veil of secrecy that had shrouded his own group's activities. Gardner, a former student of Malaysian magic, was establishing a new reputation through the study of witchcraft. Along with supervising a slew of new Ritual groups, Gardner established a Museum of Magic and Witchcraft on the Isle of Man, a place whose inhabitants, according to Gardner, possessed all of the characteristics of the "Little Town." Gardner asserted that he was merely transmitting the Knowledge, not reconstructing it. However, Sybil Leek does not accept the authenticity of the nakedness and ritual sex that characterised the meetings (as well as the dissident groups associated with Alex Sanders).

Francis King, a contemporary writer on the more trained modern occult, suggests that Gardner was limited to expressing his exhibitionist and sadomasochistic tendencies through the rites he proposed, adding that in the early 1940s, he commissioned the not-so-famous Aleister Crowley to prepare four of the rites for use in a cult of resurrected witchcraft.

The late 1950s and early 1960s were the heyday of new ritual groups, despite the enormous publicity that would eventually fragment the "Old Religion" into a hundred heresies. Sybil Leek was appointed high priestess of an association near Nice that had previously been led by an elderly Russian aunt. He then returned to his antique shop in New Forest, where he founded the ritual group Horsa. Alex Sanders, who began his witchcraft studies with his Welsh grandmother and then conducted some black magic incursions before joining one of the new groups.

Gerald Gardner was assassinated in 1964. Raymond Buckland was the man who carried on Gardner's work, particularly in the United States. He was both a writer and an editor of classic works, such as the Aradia de Leland, and he founded his own witchcraft museum on Long Island. June Johns published The King of Warlocks: The World of Alex Sanders in 1969, a year after Sybil Leek's Diary of a Witch. Stewart Farrar, a 1971 journalist, was one of those converted by Sanders's description of the term wicca. What Sorcerers Do: The Modern Nudist Ritual group, book in which he recounted his own rapid ascension to knowledge and detailed a "Alexandrian" ritual.

What remains to be told? Francis King, who shares my suspicion that modern groups of sorcerers did not emerge until Margaret Murray's first book was published, acknowledges the existence of two English groups when Gardner arrived in the New Forest. It is possible that they came to understand how they were influenced by the Book of Shadows, one of the numerous manuscripts in which the high Priestess of a ritual group is required to record the rites performed by her group. I've seen two editions of the Book of Shadows in print. One is a quite vulgar collection of enchantments akin to an occultist's manuscript. The other is a copy written by Lady Sheba, the "Queen of the American Witches," and presented by Llewellyn Publications. Lady Sheba's manual is divided into three sections: laws, rituals, and covens. The laws contain indications about how a witch should behave if she is tortured. If authentic, they would establish that Wicca laws date all the way back to the early seventeenth century.

The rites are structured in the manner that the vast majority of ritual groups do. The Wizards perform their naked rites within a nine-foot-diameter circle traced with a consecrated knife by the high priestess (athame). Within the circle is an altar equipped with everything necessary for the rites (candles, water, salt, a bell, and a rope whip). There are eight Great Covens (Sabbats), or significant festivals (for example, All Saints' Eve), and twenty-six Esbats, which correspond to the new and full moons, and each one must be observed with appropriate symbolism. In festivals where sorcerers are initiated into one of the three degrees of Knowledge, additional rites include "the five-fold kiss" (on the feet, knees, groyne, chest, and lips), a gentle flogging, and convenient admonitions.

Apart from nakedness and flogging, they are not always erotic in nature in the most serious ritual groups. There are few passages in Lady Sheba's text that would annoy the average reader. Of course, there is no mention of harming another person, which is typical of the stereotyped sorcerer. When taken at face value, the modern group rituals he describes are poetic and gentle evocations of nature's rhythm.

The Devil is well-known for his oblivion. Because any version of the Book of Shadows is inherently a product of a living tradition, it is impossible to determine how much of it is Lady Sheba's recent work and how much is pre-Gerald Gardner. Tanya informs me that her grandmother's "Black Book" was dubbed the "Book of Calls" because it contained several demonic invocations written in what appeared to be reversed Latin. This indicates that the originals of what is now known as the Book of Shadows were nothing more than magic books or black magic manuals in use since the Middle Ages, to which they had added fragments of an oral tradition concerning ritual group procedures.

This oral tradition may have begun when a lone sorcerer passed on his knowledge to another; group rules may have evolved gradually, taking those sorcerers who were ideally supposed to meet in groups for granted. However, there may never be a way to definitively determine what is and is not true about these contemporary groups. No discussion of contemporary witchcraft would be complete without mentioning Anton LaVey's purported Satanism, which believes that all traditional religions are fraudulent and psychologically destructive. LaVey converted a group of First Church of Satan members who met to discuss occultism in 1966. His house in San Francisco became the centre for Black Masses, which received widespread publicity and included all necessary components: a naked woman as an altar, theatrical invocations of the devil, and advice to practise the "seven deadly sins." LaVey, whose sense of theatricality surpasses even Alex Sanders, has established himself as a master of occult fantasy in the purest Aleister Crowleyian tradition. One of the numerous books he has written, The Satanic Bible, expresses a consistent philosophy in which the Devil is portrayed as the embodiment of all human desires suppressed by orthodox Christianity.

The Satanic Church's Devil cult seeks to satisfy a human need for rituals while also allowing for the expression therapy of sensuality and hostility that are inherent in the human condition. Witchcraft, as LaVey defined it, is a collection of techniques for enhancing latent paranormal abilities. It may be nothing more than one day up to date with Aleister Crowley's renewed "Magick," but it has not ceased to irritate other cult wizards.

The debate over whether witchcraft should be classified as a religion arose shortly after Tanya's beloved grandmother died of cancer. This one had begun to experience repeated sleep, emphasising the sense of loss that is central to the majority of theological conceptions of hell. The Loss was caused in the dream by their refusal to adopt any religious beliefs. According to your psychiatrist, who had visited you intermittently since childhood for therapy purposes, the dream indicated that Tanya had not yet confronted the uniquely religious dimension of human mortality. He struggled to make sense of his grandmother's death, both surprised and saddened. The doctor inquired as to how Tanya could claim to be a witch and not identify with any religious experience. She maintained her atheism, and the psychiatrist was equally adamant in pointing out the evidence of religious concern that sprouted from his subconscious. Finally, he had to admit that he believed in God and that this belief altered the perspective of his magic.

It is exceedingly difficult, if not impossible, to draw a distinction between magic and religion. Both speak of the world in terms that transcend the narrow confines of what we now refer to as nascent awareness, the distinction between the discovery of transcendence, to which man responds with worship, and the recognition of a harmony, which you attempt to synchronise through its symbols. From this vantage point, it makes sense that magic should continue to operate within a religious framework and that religion should benefit from adopting the robes of magic. Tanya, who has finally discovered a religious feeling, shares in this regard the position of cult witches, who have declared their rites to be intrinsically religious since the days of Gerald Gardner. Sybil Leek may have gone further in this direction; in The Artful of Witchcraft, she develops a theology for the "Ancient Religion," combining Asian concepts about nature's duality (as in the Chinese concept of Ying and Yang), karma, and the theme of lunar worship, which Aradia introduced us to.

This religious zeal demonstrates the extent to which ritual groups today are the natural heirs of previous era's moralising secret societies. Is it a religious experience compatible with the Judeo-Christian tradition? Anton LaVey mocked those who accepted the "Old Religion" for their inability to see themselves as authentic anti-Christians, but their own views are backed up by a fairly incomplete presentation of Christianity. According to Gerald Gardner, there was no conflict between being a Christian, albeit heterodox, and a witch, and I am unaware of any ritual group in their tradition that requires explicit renunciation of Christianity, which was a requirement of mediaeval legend. While these concepts may irritate many fundamentalist Christians, they are a widely held belief among sorcerers. Earlier, I stated that young people who accept witchcraft as a counterculture concept generally do not engage in religious practises.

Numerous people are willing to follow Anton LaVey and Philips Bonewits (author of Real Magic) in their wholly materialistic view of magic. However, this has not prevented the return of magic from being a religious phenomenon, in my opinion. While witchcraft is not always a complete belief system in and of itself, it is something that works in the absence of other beliefs to satisfy a specific religious need, the need for meaning in the person who transcends the limits of ordinary experience and receives a type of experience that confirms the reality of this transcendence. Religious needs are not universally strong in all people or cultures. They manifest in the most extraordinary ways when other institutional forces falter. The formation of the first ritual groups in the 1950s coincided with a dramatic increase in the church's attractiveness following the devastation of World War II and Cold War tensions. In both periods, men looked inward, and religion and magic grew in popularity concurrently.

Occultism disguised as counterculture, born of anti-Vietnam War sentiment, gained widespread acceptance in the public imagination at the same time that it began to charge into the formation of a strong and new fundamentalism, dubbed the People of Jesus. As a historian, I must point out that, despite its exquisite presentation, the legend of the "Old Religion" remains a relatively recent addition to the central flow of western occultism. However, for the most serious wizards, Wicca satisfies a genuine need, and they are the only ones who compete to determine the validity of the religious experience derived from it. Tanya may declare herself a witch today, but three centuries ago, a similar declaration in the Christian world would have resulted in an invitation to appear before local magistrates, which could involve torture or even death for committing the most heinous crime the mediaeval mind could conceive.

Naturally, this has not always been the case, nor has it been the case everywhere. For example, in Russia, there have never been the massive witchcraft persecutions that characterised Western Europe.

Tanya's grandmother once told us how they massacred nearly everyone in her village during a pogrom when she was a small child. It was unnecessary to seek out those who dealt with the Devil when the Jews were on hand to absorb the aggressions brought about by a hostile environment and an absence of documentation. And, recalling the horrors of my parenting years, Europe demonstrated an uncanny ability to resort to pogrom once more when it became necessary to find victims for the dark gods of material success.

Tanya's dual status as a witch and a Jew is purely coincidental.

The irony is that while we would still be subject to mediaeval laws, Tanya would almost certainly be acquitted of witchcraft charges because she is not a baptised Christian and thus cannot be an apostate, as a witch is defined to be. Given their knowledge of the world of magic, both in beliefs and practises, he would condemn the laws prohibiting witchcraft and could still be questioned, under torture, about the renegade Christians who attended sorcerers' "covens" and "synagogues." Although they left it amusingly open, in some regions, he may be forced to wear a head dress known as a "bean hat" as a symbol of his public misfortune.

Although modern treatises on witchcraft attribute the term "sabbat" (coven) to a romantic origin that distinguishes it from the Jewish "sabbath" (Jewish Saturday), a cursory examination of mediaeval sources indicates that this custom was imposed by crude anti-Semitism. For example, witch clusters are frequently referred to as "synagogues"; the term "coven" does not appear in the literature of the trials until the late seventeenth century in Scotland. The witch's head rides, in regions and eras where this concept was central to the image of a witch, a ritual gathering of thirteen sorcerers. Other than Herodias, the scandalous queen who obtained her daughter's head in a tray, the head of John the Baptist is frequently requested. During the sixteenth and seventeenth centuries' worst witchcraft panics, sorcerers were frequently accused of the same antisocial behaviours (poisoning, child murder) previously attributed to Jews. Finally, as with the Jews, the sorcerer is condemned not for what he does but for who he is... he who has rejected Christ.

The implicit association of Judaism with witchcraft is, in my opinion, the key to understanding the mediaeval legend of the witch, which eventually gave rise to fantasies like Aradia and Margaret Murray and Gerald Gardner's Celtic reconstructions. This also explains why there were few persecutions and no hysteria in a country like Spain, whereas Western Europe was convulsing in fear of sorcerers.

The Spanish church was far too preoccupied with the Moors, Jews, and Muslims who had converted only nominally to Catholicism in response to Fernando and Isabel's edict demanding the exile of non-Christians. In Italy, another country where the sorcerers' madness did not explode, the fear of Protestants was sufficient.

26

Although the true story is much more complicated than Margaret Murray's legend of the "Antigua Religion," there is some truth to her assertion that the Witchcraft tradition implied a pagan background. At the dawn of time, two social classes existed that were capable of resisting forced Christianization. The country's inhabitants (the pagans, according to the Latin term for a country region) transformed Catholicism into a disguise for older practises, much like the Indian and mestizo populations of Latin America today.

The other category was the educated aristocracy. Numerous non-Christian aristocrats, men of fortune and culture, resisted until the sixth century, two hundred years after Constantine, when they generally admitted as chaplains from his house the deposed professors of Greek philosophy, who had already been integrated with the remnants of the Greek religion during the early Christian era, and sent their children to philosophy schools. When the Muslim invaders destroyed what remained of the Roman Empire in the south and east, they discovered that despite Christianity's persistent efforts to suppress them, traditions of magic alchemy, astrology, and sorcery persisted.

It is worth noting that the highly intellectualised Hellenistic magic may be reintroduced to Western Europe via Islam. Two issues have arisen among the population of remote rural areas. There was always resistance to new practises, and the threat of relapse into heretical beliefs was partially mitigated by the church taking over the festivities, "baptising" local divinities ("San" Cristóbal or "San" Jorge) and adopting old customs (decorating a fir tree for Christmas or eggs for Easter). The orgiastic fertility rites were not easily assimilated, and in older literature, pastors were reprimanded for encouraging such holidays.

The other issue, which proved to be the most challenging, was the appeal of heretics or visionaries to a populace that was already

27

beginning to resent the Catholic clergy's power and privileges. More formidable than reformers such as the Waldensians, whom they relocated from Lyon to Italy, was the dualistic orientation of Persian Zoroastrianism (the idea that good and evil, light and darkness, spirit and matter, and God and the Devil are realities other than a struggle for men's souls) that prevailed in many of the groups opposed to the new Christian church. Mani, the Persian prophet, used dualism to structure a church in the century, following the Catholic hierarchy's lines, and its philosophy (Manichaeism) was preserved through a series of mediaeval movements that they included.

The Dominican order was originally founded to counter the Cathars' influence through more effective preaching, and the combative attitude of those priests was a major factor in the persecution of witches following the Cathars' annihilation. The rural populace, who could barely retain the subtleties of Orthodox theology correctly, could not avoid a certain distortion of heresy. A protest against the church's wealth, for example, could devolve into a 'bloody uprising against all who had assumed power in the name of Christ'.

There were genuine devil worshippers in isolated areas of mediaeval Europe, and this was based on the later development of the legend of witchcraft. The church was incapable of appreciating the extent to which the survival of pagan forms combined with the influence of heresies such as the Cathars ("the purified ones") to give rise to the belief in sorcerers.

Every act of sorcery, no matter how trivial, was regarded as diabolical by the most orthodox theologians, and the coexistence of popular magic and true diabolism resulted in an understandable identification. He also fostered an ecclesiastical paranoia that persisted until the usual reasons for fearing Witchcraft, such as epidemics or devastating storms, failed to materialise. However, this identification was insufficient. The old anti-paganism sentiment and the new fear of heresy resulted in an odd contradiction even within their own Church documents. At a time when the church was busy degrading traditional practises, an ordinance appeared in Charlemagne's court denouncing the popular belief that women rode in the skies following the goddess Diana's hosts.

According to this Canon Episcopi, priests were required to explain that such a ride was a deception concocted by the Devil to divert Christians' attention away from their faith in God as the sole source of miraculous power. By misinterpretation of the collection of decrees that included the Canon Episcopi in the tenth century, it was assumed that it originated at the Council of Ancyra in the fourth century and thus possessed the force of a dogma. When taken literally, it appeared to condemn one of the central beliefs of so many subsequent persecutors: the miraculous transportation of sorcerers to remote regions where they celebrated their "covens." The unaffected defenders of the proposition that sorcerers performed those night flights insisted on a distinction between the pagans mentioned in the Canon Episcopi and a new and more dangerous sect, a cult of sorcerers that began in the early fifteenth century.

The fact that theologians continued to debate the details of witchcraft may have contributed to the decline of mass trials at the end of the eighteenth century, but it rarely aided those charged with witchcraft. The sorcerer was condemned for his being, not for his actions. It was blasphemous for the church to indulge in an orgy entirely fictitious method of attending such jaranas personally. If we remember that sorcery was punishable even in pagan Rome, we will have a better understanding of how judgments accepted near the end of the Roman Empire could become a legalised butcher shop of gigantic proportions over the course of several centuries,

29

an avalanche that ended with the final doubts about personal freedom.

The tragic thing was that public opinion and hysteria subsided only after this had occurred. How many people died prior to that?

Numerous writers accept the exaggerated figures of extremely jealous pursuers and speak of nine million deaths; the horrifying figure of two hundred thousand appears to be more accurate. The legend of witchcraft as a distinct evil from sorcery gained momentum in the eighth century. In 1022, in the French city of Orleans, a heresy trial was held in which sexual orgies and cannibalism were cited as charges against Christians, which the Romans had already used against Christians and Christians against Jews.

Additionally, there was talk of instant transport to obscene rituals in which the Devil would manifest as a black man. In 1335, the Inquisition held in Toulouse and Carcassonne, both of which were former centres of heresy, rendered several notable judgments for two reasons. The first is the use of the term "sabbat" to refer to specific days of worship; the second is the use of torture to elicit the necessary confessions in order for the church to deliver the suspects to the state, "the secular arm," for execution. After half a century, the trials' proceedings and charges were not as frequent as some wished.

Indeed, it almost always appeared as though local law enforcement officials were unaware of the enormity of the diabolic conspiracy that had existed since the fifteenth century, and it was necessary to rouse an enthusiastic pursuer.

It appears to have been a rather ruthless man who had made friends with very powerful people in Rome and obtained a papal appointment as inquisitor for southern Germany through them in 1474. In 1476, Institutoris were swept up in the witch-hunter frenzy but frequently found themselves constrained by the procedural requirements that limited the Inquisition's scope. Ten years after his appointment, Institutoris obtained a document from Pope Innocent VIII granting him and his inquisitor comrade, Jacob Sprenger, complete authority for the witch hunt, thus freeing his peculiar ecclesiastical court from the constraints imposed by magistrates and more conservative bishops. Two more years later, Institutoris \spersuaded Sprenger, who was also a professor of theology in \sCologne, to lend his name as co-author of a new treaty, Malleus \sMaleficarum (The Hammer of Warlocks), with which Institutoris \shoped to recover part of the reputation lost because of its excesses.

Not content with obtaining Sprenger's collaboration, Institutoris also created the appearance (apparently through forgery) that the work was endorsed by the prestigious Cologne theological faculty, when in fact only four professors were willing to accept their extremism. It was not long before Institutoris and Sprenger had a disagreement, which appeared to be reasonable, and eventually, after the Dominicans expelled him from Germany, the pope assigned Institutoris a new mission in Eastern Europe. The tragedy is that the Malleus, having been reprinted numerous times and being a stylish book of mediaeval discussions, became the standard reference for anyone interested in seeing sorcerers in his backyard. Skeptics found it easier to disregard that refutation... after all, it had been printed with a papal seal and a letter of approval from the renowned faculty of Cologne, both of which were capable of intimidating anyone.

The most delectable section of the book is the discussion of the belief that demons can act as sexual partners (the incubus and succubus) and how women, given their perversity and insatiable lust, were willing to accept the pleasures of those demonic loves. While it's self-evident that a woman desiring sexual contact with a fallen angel is capable of the most heinous crimes, Institutoris specialised in painting his passion for abortion and infant sacrifice, which was later used against numerous unfortunate midwives during periods of hysteria. Additionally, sorcerers could not only induce impotence (a curious recurring theme in all primitive literature about witchcraft), but they could also simulate castration in the unfortunate men they faced. All of this, on top of the usual disasters of bad weather and poor harvests. It is worth noting that the term "synagogue" is omitted, most likely because it has not yet gained currency in the popular German translation with which Institutoris was more familiar, but possibly also because it could have been counterproductive. The Inquisition, as envisioned by that sexually obsessed Dominican, piqued my interest in discovering women who had sexual relations with demons and agreed to act as instruments for the destruction of their Christian neighbours in order to continue their infernal loves.

As a result, any personal setbacks, particularly sexual in nature, should be sufficient to persuade a "witness," whose anonymity was protected throughout the trial, to denounce a witch.

As HR Trevor-Roper noted in his own analysis of the period, the witch hunts merely inherited the logic of the pogroms that had ravaged the same part of Germany at the turn of the century in which the Malleus appeared. The references to a "witch race" are particularly disturbing, as they imply that what may have been a voluntary transgression on the part of the parents became a metaphysical stigma in the son, which could be used calmly to justify the genocide. Brother Heinrich is a frightening example of the type of hysteria that can ensue whenever a strange conspiracy is rumoured. If there were a priest in the modern era, we would find him rallying local Knights of Colon members against communist threat and writing exhaustively documented analyses of the subversive messages contained in rock music. The Inquisition, which was normally a research body, received a white letter from the pope, and Institutoris taught the West how to hunt sorcerers with deadly efficiency. The French and German documents of the subsequent two centuries attest to how communities repeatedly decimate themselves and then reject their actions with horror.

The Malleus portrayed witches as sexual predators, and as HC Erick Midelfort notes in his own work on witch hunts, it was precisely during this period that he began to undermine the ancient concept of marriage, resulting in an increase in the number of single women who could raise the suspicions of the officers in charge. When the hunt began, single women were not the only victims or unfaithful, as each victim was required to confess to the Devil who else had surrendered. They drew up lists of men, women, children, and the elderly. The innkeepers and midwives faced the greatest risk of being named in the initial round of accusations, but owners and businessmen quickly followed. Dissenting law enforcement officials, particularly those who objected to those judicial proceedings, were also easy targets for their colleagues, but frequently one of the pursuers became entangled in its own network. The confession of the persecutor, perhaps named by vengeful suspects, used to be a precursor to a final panic attack before the community recognised the absurdity of his posture.

Even after this, it took years for the factionalism created by the judgments to dissipate, and factionalism within the reigning burn could still spark a new witch hunt. And this is being done in the name of religion and public order!

It is critical to remember that, contrary to what we know about Heinrich Institutoris, the majority of trials in Europe were not initiated by the Inquisition, which paid scant attention to the extensive Malleus Maleficarum. The divisions that resulted from the Protestant Reformation in Christianity only served to reinforce the French and German communities' conviction that the Devil was indeed intervening in human events in a new and frightening way.

Protestants and Catholics, despite their disagreements on doctrinal points, agreed that those who made a covenant with Satan committed the worst human crime, something so heinous and concealed that it justified the use of extraordinary measures to discover it.

No malicious act or physical assistance to a coven was as significant to the continental persecutors as the fact that someone had abandoned his baptismal vows out of lust or greed to become the devil's prey. One of the most enduring ironies of the judgments is the acceptance of confessions as reliable indicators of the extent of diabolic activity within a community. Witches repeatedly admitted to being duped by the Father of Lies, either because the gold he promised them became earthenware or because demonic loves were more painful than pleasing. Even the covens had to be regarded as fictitious. However, when one person, regardless of age or position, is accused of witchcraft, several suspects are forced to confront the torturers.

A suspect almost never deviated from the expected course of action, and the circumstances surrounding their confession were used to reject any subsequent retraction. The only other option - which would have been completely unacceptable to those pious men - would have been to admit that the judgments themselves were false. Thus far, we have discussed the development of the witchcraft legend in regions of Europe where the Cathars and Jews had already been persecuted. Among the numerous theories about how witchcraft became mad at the end of the fifteenth century, Trevor-Roper chose the idea that he embodied the perennial conflict between the plains' villagers and the mountain population, which was generally of different racial origin. Midelfort sees it as a result of the dislocations caused in part by the late Middle Ages' socioeconomic changes and in part by the Reformation's conflicts between Catholics and Protestants. And, of course, there are the long-dormant theories that the judgments were the result of clerical sexual frustrations or persecutor anxiety about confiscating the damned's property.

What we must remember is that the mediaeval concept of the witch evolved over centuries. Initially, it was the standard ugly old woman riding a broom with a demon in the form of a cat or toad at her side. This stereotype was completely destroyed in the sixteenth century. It was believed that the Devil could buy anyone's worship during this new and dangerous era.

For example, the great astronomer Kepler was powerless to prevent his own mother's arrest for witchcraft; she died in prison prior to the trial, perhaps fortunately for her. At the turn of the century, a group of Ursuline nuns from a convent in Loudun demonstrated demonic possession, and an unpopular priest, Urban Grandier, was executed in the same manner as the sorcerer who had sold their souls to the devil. Yes, Satan was present everywhere, including within the church. While I concur with Midelfort's theory that witch hunts in general reflected an insecurity as the mediaeval era gave way to the modern era, a witch hunt could also occur simply because a community, aware of the devil's presence everywhere, discovered evidence of an attack by the devil.

What occurred in Salem, Massachusetts colony, is an excellent example. Fewer than fifty people were executed in America on witchcraft charges, but twenty of them were from Salem during the horrifying panic of 1692. To comprehend Salem, it is necessary to acknowledge that, during the sixteenth and seventeenth centuries, England and its colonies appeared to be far less concerned about witchcraft than continental Europe.

For example, there was never a concern for heresy, as was the case with continental judgments, and torture was never used to extract the type of confessions that have perpetuated witch hunts in France and Germany.

-

Chadwick Hansen's book, Witchcraft in Salem, is a late attempt to exonerate the Massachusetts Puritan leaders, particularly Cotton Mather, from the charges levelled against them by unsympathetic chroniclers. According to him, certain blunders in the field of divination resulted in hysterical reactions among a gang of teenagers. When one of the women accused by the girls (Tituba, a Caribbean Indian slave) freely confessed his diabolism, the initial accusation of witchcraft appeared justified. The subsequent investigations revealed evidence that others who were later tried had engaged in witchcraft, even black magic, but this alone would not have distinguished Salem - or its judgments - from any other American or English community.

What distinguished Salem was the courts' decision to accept "spectral evidence" - the girls' descriptions of how they "saw" several community members attempting malicious actions against them - over Cotton Mather's publicly expressed opinion, which had previously successfully treated cases of similar hysteria.

Because hysteria is mediated by attention, a certain number of men and women were charged, convicted, and executed before judges recognised that the multiplying accusations, which quickly reached the community's most influential citizens, had to be false. This shift in perspective trampled on the phenomena that precipitated the trials, and Salem's experience influenced the renewal of English laws, effectively putting an end to such persecutions. The sorcerers may still be apprehended, but only in the capacity of imposters.

Salem has developed into a tourist destination for those interested in seeing the relics of that somewhat obscure period of American history. Some episodes of the Bewitched television series were filmed there in order to combine old and new legends, the mediaeval conception of the witch as a Satanist and the Hollywood version, in a sort of amusing superset. However, the truth is that something heinous occurred there, and no amount of laughter could undo the damage done in the name of God and the Crown. All those comrades regarding witches as Devil's consorts fell out of favour with the advent of a new scientific mentality. The judgments themselves had begun to wane even before that, as he realised, as was the case in Salem, that the law was not the best vehicle for dealing with what people referred to as the supernatural.

Additionally, as Trevor-Roper noted, a general trend toward less use of torture as an interrogation technique resulted in fewer confessions, and the fewer confessions, the lower the likelihood of new ones.

However, in regions where ancient beliefs die slowly, such as the rural Devonshire area that Tanya vividly recalls, fear of witchcraft may continue to fuel violence. Doreen Brave recounts the story of a Devonshire farmer who assaulted a woman whom he accused of witchcraft with his pig. Your intentions had been to draw blood in order to break the spell and to threaten her with death. That was in 1924, but I have no doubt that the same views still hold true today. Tanya was fortunate not to discuss her witchcraft with her classmates when she was a child attending that region's school. She, too, could have been a victim of an attack. Even now, we continue to use pseudonyms, as we cannot be certain that someone, somewhere, will not blame her for any private setbacks she may be experiencing. George Santayana, an American philosopher, once stated that men who ignore history are doomed to repeat their lessons. He has a sneaking suspicion that the converse is also true.

Often, we require current experience in order to comprehend the meaning of the past. The witch hunts of the late Middle Ages can be thought of as a subset of the great spy hunts that occur whenever towns become fearful of subversion by a powerful and cunning adversary. However, the psychology that generated them would remain unchanged, even if a new metaphysics were to replace the old. As Arthur Miller suggested in his novel The Crucible, the fear of sabotage has remained relatively constant, regardless of whether the setting is seventeenth-century Salem or modern-day Washington. Only gods and devils are distinct. One of the least pleasant aspects of spying is how patriots' behaviour mimics the alleged image of the enemy. We have, for example, the John Birch Society and the Minutemen, which are a carbon copy of the Communist Party of the Soviet Union's most heinous characteristics.

The same can be said of Greece's, Brazil's, and South Vietnam's dictatorships when we read about tactics such as indiscriminate arrests and frequently lethal torture used to thwart a real or imagined communist threat. In England, where the most macabre aspects of hunting for continental sorcerers were generally ignored, one of the most heinous characters who brought the widespread fear of witchcraft to the fore was a dark lawyer named Mattew Hopkins, who, beginning in 1644, terrorised Essex County with a pretendissue issued by Parliament, where he was appointed General Discoverer of Warlocks. He charged a fee for his services and demonstrated considerable skill in obtaining confessions, despite laws prohibiting the torture of suspects. Hopkins, who once claimed to be in possession of the Devil's payroll of althea witches in England (imagine standing before a people's court and declaring, "I have a list"), based his image of the sorcerer on a volume written by King James I shortly before his ascension to the throne of United England and Scotland.

Jacobo intended Demonology to serve as a replica for sceptics such as Reginald Scot, author of The Discovery of Witchcraft, and it brutalised the European witch's image as the Devil's lover. The Statutes of 1604, which were approved one year after Jacobo arrived in England, expanded the definition of witchcraft and strengthened the penalties that should be applied. The king was gradually losing faith, particularly after witnessing a clear case of fraudulent spell, but his book and its laws were plagued by a later period. They proved to be a fast track to fame and fortune for Essex's lawyer. Hopkins spent two years hunting women whose pets could be taken by demons sent to advise them on their hexes, as described in Demonology. Along with the psychological torture of the continuous twenty-four-hour interrogation, he revived a mediaeval ordeal for a suspected witch: throw her into a stream of water to see if she floated or sank, assuming the Devil would protect his servant from drowning. It was not long before their activities were halted by higher authorities, but if old statistics are to be believed, Hopkins was responsible for several hundred executions before being called to account for his illegal procedures and the benefits he obtained from his witch persecution.

One of the most perplexing aspects of the entire witch hunt period is that, similar to how fear of communist terror can be used to justify extraordinary political repression, fear of magic was one of the factors that induced citizens who would otherwise fear God to submit to those practises prohibited in self-defense. Doreen Brave, for example, speaks of a glass-covered box believed to have been sold by Hopkins as a means of protection against witches and containing some of the materials associated with witchcraft. What people accepted as normal, apart from sermons on the inherent evil of sorcery that they should hear in their parish church, was that witchcraft existed... and appeared to work. Following the same mental process as the good Christians who borrowed money from Shylock in Shakespeare's The Merchant of Venice, it could be condemned to engage in a particular type of activity without profiting from it.

For example, when European Christians discovered that Jews were "useful" and the only ones willing to deal with the prohibited but necessary monetary loan practises in England, one factor that mitigated the witch hunt was that nobody, except the most fanatical pursuers, desired to eliminate all sorcerers out of fear of remaining defenceless against a new attack by the Spirit of Evil. According to Jeffrey Burton Russell, a historian who places the origins of witchcraft madness in previous centuries' beliefs and practises, only 20% of witchcraft charges contained "theological refinements." The remainder was derived from popular tradition, which theologians, including men like Institutoris, preferred to learn rather than invent.

This is the tradition to which we must devote our attention if we are to penetrate the legends of old and new witchcraft, to ascertain the truth about witches in the past and how this can assist us in comprehending the possibility of magic in the present.

The Reality of Sorcerers

We have examined two legends: Margaret Murray's reconstruction of the "Old Religion" and contemporary ritual groups; and the mediaeval image of the devil, which was trampled by jealous persecutors who went beyond the bounds of civil and ecclesiastical law.

Although Tanya rejects the ritual group as a vehicle for its own magic and believes it does not fit the image of a devil's consort, she continues to refer to herself as a witch. In this regard, I have encouraged her and others, primarily because I am unable to think of a more appropriate term and because it implies a sense of tradition that I believe is necessary for effective magic.

What, then, is the true story of those we now refer to as sorcerers? Due to the fact that the legends we have discussed thus far have always originated in a European environment, I will confine the following considerations to the West, specifically to Celtic sources. Later, we will discuss the meaning of magic in non-

41

Western terms, but for now, suffice it to say that there are few aspects of African, Asian, or American tradition that are significantly different from those of Oldest Europe. Europe itself can be envisioned as a beach to which they have been washed away by successive tides, each depositing new materials. We know very little about the first, as the majority of our archaeological evidence and written history are a product of the subsequent waves. However, as we approach the second millennium, we can now more precisely locate these metaphorical tides.

Certain peoples, such as the Achaeans and Etruscans, developed civilizations that rivalled those of Egypt and Syria, with which they traded, but they eventually melted away as new villages were pushed north of the Black Sea. The Greeks and Romans conquered the northern Mediterranean peninsulas; the Iranians and Aryans conquered the Middle East and the Indian subcontinent, and the Celts conquered Western Europe in its entirety. Again, contact with the Egyptians and Phoenicians of Syria provided those new people with culture, which quickly brought them on par with the Egyptians and Phoenicians.

The Greeks used the Phoenician alphabet to preserve the memory of their cousins and Achaean forefathers in an unmatched literature, as well as to convert a decadent Egyptian theology into the remarkable new vision of man found in Pythagoras and Plato's philosophies. The Romans, like the Greeks, were great organisers; they destroyed the power of Phenicia (the Etruscans' former ally) in its colony of Carthage, north of Africa, and then advanced, first annexing Greece and then the rest of the Mediterranean. However, the organisation is not without flaws. The Romans, who were forced to contend with the threat of a Celtic invasion, were being pushed south by their Teutonic relatives. They developed an appreciation for their adversaries' worth. In stark contrast to the indulgence that seemed to be a natural outcome of their success, they saw the Celts as people who lived in close proximity to nature and with a great deal more honesty in their personal relationships.

For example, Julius Caesar wrote about the Druids, the Celtic priests, referring to them as philosophers who inspired Gallic warriors to new heights of bravery through a vision of reincarnation; and Tacitus, a century later, spoke of the Celtic exploits in what would convert the primitive version of the Noble Wild myth.

The writers of the eighteenth and nineteenth centuries accepted two contradictory versions of the Celts: those of authentic primitive beings and those of their mystical nature. As a result, a plethora of meaningless works predated Margaret Murray and Gerald Gardner's romanticism and resulted in the emergence of reconstructed druidic orders, even before ritual groups were rebuilt. The truth about the Celtic religion, which I accept alongside the truth about the first European sorcerers, is that it reflected a culture that was far less barbaric than Tacitus claims, but also far less sophisticated than Caesar intends. The Celts had already established contact with other cultures through trade with the Etruscans, and shortly before the Christian era, they found themselves in a position comparable to that of the Indian tribes confronted by English settlers on the Atlantic coast.

There were sufficient villages and communications to permit the formation of a new national unity, but the process remained incomplete. Similarly to how the European invasion prevented the Iroquois from establishing a unique power in North America, the Roman invasion destroyed the various Celtic peoples' nascent nationalism. One of the pivotal battles of this conflict occurred in Anglesey in the year 61, when Roman Paulino was subjected to a British Druid centre, despite the efforts of women dressed in black screaming for their troops to withdraw. The extent to which the Druids were powerful in England is unknown. There is no evidence linking the Druids to the ruins of Stonehenge, for example, and, despite Caesar's assumption that his centre was in England, it was possible that he did little to attract them from the continent. What we do know is that they established a priestly house in Gaul, where warriors enjoyed the privileges of a heroic aristocracy. It is entirely possible that the uniformity of a ritual education, over a period of up to two decades, would have developed in Druids a sensitivity to interests that transcended the tribes' limited concerns.

One factor that may have aided the Druids in achieving Celtic unity was the cult of Cernunos ("The Cuckold"), which enjoyed widespread acceptance. Traditionally, this pastoral divinity was depicted with antennae or horns and accompanied by a deer and a ram-headed snake. Cernunos is described in legends as the lord of animals. This god is depicted in Celtic art squatting among several animals. Additionally, he appears as lord of the underworld, providing wealth for his worshipers. For the Romans, it was critical to suppress the Druidic cult of Cernunos for purely political reasons. The Horned God will face new and obstinate adversaries with the advent of Christianity. Cernunos's squatting image was adopted as a symbol for the Devil, and the stories in which Cernunos appeared as the colossal black lord of beasts became part of folklore about how the Devil was perceived by his followers.

It should be noted that the black colour was used to symbolise the supernatural; the Celts used the colour red to symbolise death. Cernunos had a better reputation among Christians than other gods and goddesses.

The best example is the triple Brigantia (the High), or Brgida, a Celtic mother goddess who was frequently equated with Minerva by the Romans and became Santa Brigantia de Kildare. Other deities' attributes were ascribed to eminent saints, such as the monk Columba, who was said to understand bird language and to possess a white horse that foretold his owner's demise. Minor local divinities, such as figures originally revered as Protectors of wells and rivers, evolved into the fairies, which theologians defined as minor demons or unbaptized souls. Even great pastoral festivals, such as Samuin (November 1), were Christianized and renamed All Saints Day.

According to Roman accounts, the Druids engaged in animal and human sacrifices, and we know that the Celtic religion was most commonly expressed through the cult of the severed head. However, there is no evidence to support Margaret Murray's claim that Celtic priests practised the cult of Cernunos by dressing in his likeness, nor is there evidence for the existence of ritual groups of sorcerers as a form of religious bureaucracy. Cernunos is also occasionally depicted naked as the god of war (the Celts fought naked against their enemy battleships), but there is no reason to believe that Celtic festivals required participants to carry no more than "the layer of heaven." The bloody festivals of wandering bands of warriors do not fit well with the image of the coven that eventually developed in mediaeval tradition, and it appears that the image of the "synagogue" or "coven" is a strictly clerical invention comprising 20% of the tradition of witchcraft.

Even the number thirteen, which is associated with the term "coven," refers to a ritual group of thirteen sorcerers. Not to be forgotten is that the term is merely a variant of the word "convent." How I needed to know the Scottish witch who coined the term in his confession, religious groups such as the Franciscans preferred to keep their communities or convents as close to the number of Jesus and his twelve apostles as possible. No one was ever assigned a specific composition for "synagogues" during mediaeval trials. Although the transformation from human to animal form via enchantment is a recurring motif in Greco-Roman mythology. Among the Celts, this is a fundamental feature of a doctrine in

45

which the worlds of birds and animals and men constantly intersect.

It is also the source of the Celts' shared belief in vampirism with the Greeks and Romans. The warrior goddesses, particularly those who took the form of crows, were capable of attacking their adversaries and literally tearing them apart. In Greece, they were referred to as lamiai; in Rome, they were referred to as lamiae or strigae (derived from the word that was used to designate an owl). Later tradition attempted to de-ghettoize these supernatural beings by portraying them as ghost blood suckers attempting to reclaim their lost vitality. What had been a terrifying aspect of pagan goddesses became one of the accusations levelled against the elderly helpless who fit the witch's first stereotype during the Christian era. The witch's cauldron, which any Macbeth reader will recognise, is another example of Celtic folklore reduced to a manageable scale.

There are references in myths to a cauldron of immortality. Additionally, and given the Celts' reverence for water above all other elements, it was natural that cubes and cauldrons played a role in their conception of a good spell. "Bulle and bubble, labour and perplex."

Although the Druids' worldly power was defeated in their battles with the Romans, they survived for several centuries during the Christian era by transmitting knowledge lies that, even in purely secular terms, the local lords considered superior to the instruction of the first Christian priests they encountered.

The development of an order of highly intellectualised monks in Scotland, beginning with Columba in the sixth century, meant that the Druids, who were already on the verge of extinction, would lose the advantage that their poetry provided them against Christian priests who were familiar with Latin and Greek literature.

The myth became folklore that Christians appropriated for their own ends, and the magic of the gods and goddesses was infantilized, only to resurface as a collection of rural superstitions about healing and divination. Witchcraft was not yet a source of Christian fear. Quite the contrary.

Charlemagne, who established the new Holy Roman Empire on Christmas Day 800, reinforced prohibitions against belief in ancient magic, such as the Canon Episcopi, which we have already discussed.

True sorcerers - beings capable of performing marvellous feats solely through their own abilities - could not exist and did not exist. Despite these official denials, there was a Germanic folklore that contained echoes of a less settled era's walking troops of warriors. According to these legends, a spirit, typically a goddess named Perchta or Holda, who was identified with the Roman Diana, led a horde of spirits on a wild hunt, destroying everything in their path. With time, those supernatural hunters were accepted as real people endowed with the ability to fly by the goddess - the belief that the Canon was attempting to suppress Episcopi. But in a short period of time, belief in Diana gave way to belief in the Devil, and one of the components of the myth of the coven was established when the medieval clergy decided that Satan had the power to instantly transport his followers to any place.

After all, Diana doesn't know it existed, and the heresy that rejected the Canon Episcopi was to attribute to a deity Pagans wonderful powers.

The Devil was now a completely different creature, and heresy consisted in denying its capability rather than affirming it. It was always assumed that the Devil was not a self-contained entity of God. According to Christians, Satan's attacks were to be viewed as proof that the Lord had spoiled the righteous. The Book of Jacob

47

served as the foundational text in this case. The Wizards - individuals who accepted Satan's mandates for whatever reason - committed treason against the true lord of the world, despite the fact that the orgies to which wizards attended were pure hallucinations, a ruse devised by the Devil to catch the wicked. At this point, legend and history come together in an unusual way. You can read stories of voluntary confessions over and over again in the Judgment literature, where suspects claimed to have assisted the covens, even when there was evidence that they had been sleeping.

For those who believed in malevolent witches, this introduced the concept of "spectral evidence," as in the Salem trials, where those who committed evil acts were the accused's astral bodies. However, for sceptics, it provided an opportunity to comment on the peculiar properties of sorcerer's ointments. Given that aconite, belladonna, and hemlock are among the drugs mentioned in traditional recipes for flying and changing shape, sceptics were justified in asserting that the witches' only "trips" were caused by the ointments.

To my mind, the issue is determining the extent to which they were used. Except for Margaret Murray and her followers, almost all historians of witchcraft agree that the voluntary confessions described in the subject's literature are the result of mental disorders. For example, the fantastic descriptions of covens have been interpreted as hysterical responses to the mediaeval world's coldness and repression. However, it is possible that they were manifestations of a drug subculture, rooted either in ancient times or in the most recent experiments of people dubbed rural pharmacologists. With great trepidation, I venture this hypothesis.

In The Sacred Mushroom and the Cross, John M. Allegro boldly asserted that much of the ancient world's mythology, including the stories of the Old and New Testaments, reflects a cult of drugs and fertility centred on the hallucinogenic mushroom Amanita (called in agaric Europe). Allegro asserts that this cult was still active in the first century of the Christian era.

The nation's authorities; the Christian community, unaware of the sect's true origins, accepted documents such as the gospels and epistles on their face value, rather than as initiation into the cult's secret code.

Following that truth were heretics such as the Gnostics, but they were cruelly suppressed over time. I disagree with Allegro's fundamental thesis, but I must admit that I could. In the ancient world, there was an underground drug cult. It is possible that the foundations of poisons, which were once associated with witchcraft in the old imperial order, will include the science of how to use those substances in small doses or through external application to induce hallucinogenic effects. This science was capable of being transmitted within a very restricted and formal organisation and arriving relatively intact until the Middle Ages. Regardless of whether the ability to create hallucinogens was relatively ancient or relatively recent, it appears to have existed in the Middle Ages.

They were able to provide the basis for private reveries that, in a state of abnormal consciousness, could assume the form of a "separate reality" that was completely satisfactory.

This may be a much less spiritual experience than the ecstasy sanctioned by the mediaeval church, but it was extremely useful for the men and women who lived on the margins of Middle Ages society. And what about the recipes' most repulsive ingredients, such as baby fat or children's bone marrow? While they are most likely demonologists' fantasies, they could also be individuals who accepted the need for useful substances and in some cases committed infanticide or tomb rape to obtain them.

I reiterate that all of this is pure conjecture. I am only interested in this aspect of mediaeval sorcerers as adherents of a drug cult because I am aware of the role that these substances have played in the occult in more recent times.

Aleister Crowley shocked his Golden Dawn colleagues by accepting opium and cocaine as legitimate adjuvants in the practise of magic, and the resurgence of more autonomous witchcraft toward the end of the 1960s is inextricably linked to youth drug use. The same thing might have happened in the Middle Ages.

Celtic religion thrived in an environment where he drank excessively, and the Greek Dionysian cult - which was also a secret religion that coexisted with the most respectable temple cults - demanded alcohol as a means of ecstasy. Couldn't the same mode of operation have been used for even less orthodox groups in the worlds of Greek and Celtic magic? Even if there is evidence to support this hypothesis, it is worth noting that Greek beliefs and practises were so desperate that there was nothing that resembled universal worship. For example, the poet Robert Graves has expressed the opposing view that there was a cult of the "White Goddess" throughout ancient Europe and, following Margaret Murray, that mediaeval witch ritual groups maintained this cult until a later period.

Of course, a lunar motif exists in Greek folklore, in the triplicity of Artemis-Selene-Hecate (the crescent moon, the full moon, and the waning moon), and Celtic representations of a mother goddess (the Magna Mater) resemble this Greek image. However, the Celts were once proponents of triads. Additionally, unlike their Greek counterparts, Celtic mother goddesses are occasionally depicted with attributes that identify them as goddesses of the hunt – a critical aspect of the Diana cult, as interpreted by members of Modern ritual groups. If not even the Druids, Cernunos' servants, appeared in the entire Celtic world, the existence of an extended matriarchal cult dedicated to Diana's Celtic counterpart seems improbable.

I tend to agree with Jeffrey Burton Russell's assessment of the mediaeval image of the witch as a gradual humanization of the ancient Celtic deities' characteristics. There is no doubt that the Celtic world was rife with sorcery. Regardless of the arts practised by tribal shamans, they are collectively referred to as druids. I believe that this witchcraft survived the Druids' demise and was already being preached by Christian priests. Its practitioners were almost certainly mostly women, who were excluded from Druidic and Christian ministries. During the Middle Ages, those witches who were forced to keep their secret practises secret due to prohibitions would be Christians, but with strong Celtic overtones.

As with Haiti's voodoo, the language of sorcery had to change to reflect the official beliefs that supplanted the more primitive religion of a subjugated people, but witchcraft itself referred to a mythical structure culled from an almost forgotten era. Ironically, and as was the case in Haiti, the customs of a vanished priesthood would be preserved by individuals who were previously barred from such ministry. Thus, it is correct to speak of "Old Religion," but not precisely in the way Margaret Murray interprets it. It is obvious that numerous other influences played a role in the development of Middle Ages witchcraft. By introducing a Cathar vision of the world through the legend developed by the persecutors, he was able to convince the sorcerers to replace Cernunos with the Devil, in his memory of a Celtic past. Although he viewed the Devil as a friend of humanity in these circumstances, rather than as his implacable adversary.

Another influence was the tradition of ceremonial magic, which was reintroduced to the West by those familiar with its continuity in the Islamic world's hybrid culture. The magical texts, for example, were a clear cup of Celtic witchcraft, even though the magicians, who were typically urban men and intellectuals, interpreted their sorcery as a manipulation of hidden natural powers, not as the erotic cult of the devil ascribed to ignorant peasants. However, over time, fragments of science from those treaties may have merged with Celtic practises, reinforcing the image of the sorcerer as possessed by demonic forces. Meanwhile, a potentially condemnatory element had been introduced into the tradition of witchcraft's permissible and prohibited activities. It was the notion that a sorcerer's soul could detach itself from his body in order to aid covens.

The Lamia or Striga concept from Greco-Roman folklore was applied to all sorcerers. It was no longer about changing shape, as in lycanthropy, but about the sorcerer's astral or spectral body's insidious action. Even with this understanding, there was a conviction that demoniacs were people possessed by strange powers worshipped by sorcerers. Through exorcism ceremonies, the haunted may be compelled to reveal the source of the evil that has afflicted him. He may even be able to see what happened to the sorcerer's Spectral body, regardless of the location or activities of your physical body.

In the 1630s, in Loudun, a hysterical French prioress, Soeur Jeanne des Anges, convinced enough people that she was possessed to precipitate the arrest of a priest, Urban Grandier, who had earned the enmity of the town's leading citizens. Throughout the trial, the judges heard testimony confirming that the priest, despite his imprisonment, was still capable of attacking the nuns in their convent.

Grandier was tortured and then burned alive after being condemned by sorcier (sorcerer). Soeur Jeanne, whose frantic retraction had been cited by the judges as further evidence of the severity of his possession, was finally delivered from his demons and became something of a celebrity at Louis XIII's court. The future

Louis XIV, the king's son, was born wearing the nun's shirt, which was said to be miraculous.

Prior to that, we will examine the complex tradition that developed in the Mediterranean world during the Druids' decline.

In the following chapters, we will delve deeper into the world of Hellenistic magic, which is the source of the vast majority of knowledge that sorcerers accept as inheritance without questioning its true origin.

It is astrology and alchemy's world, as well as the world of ceremonial magic. It transcends Tanya's world and the Celts' "elf arts." And I believe that through his work, we can begin to understand something else about the true nature of occultism, its role in the development of Western thought, including even the scientific point of view, which by definition appears to be diametrically opposed to everything that is understood by magic.

In Wicca, The Myths Are Created

Nobody knows where Wicca's myths originate; the only certainty is that they originated with the ancient Celts, who invented stories about actual events or made up fanciful stories in order to pass on their beliefs from generation to generation. The majority of myths are primarily descriptions of the actions of the gods and other significant religious figures. There is no such thing as a unique and true book of myths, because mythology is a personal experience for wiccans, whether alone or in a circle, with the gods.

Among the mythologies, the most well-known is that of Merlin, which is familiar to even those who do not practise the ancient religion. The majority of the symbols in our rituals originate from these myths, as they are a representation of all of Wicca's myths and beliefs. This will become clearer as we study the Sabbats.

What we should remember in relation to Wicca is that we ALL have the ability to write our own myths and beliefs about the gods. There is no conception since wicca is not a religion of the book, but rather a religion of personal EXPERIENCE with the gods.

THE DEITIES

Similarly, we recognise that there are stereotypes about deities, but this is not because they are the only accepted conception of them that distinguishes us from other world religions. Wicca has its own unique conception of the gods, and above all, it has the freedom to worship any of the gods, taking on the persona of the god with whom you feel most at ease. Regarding what we refer to as gods, there are several common names known to the majority of pagans, each one assigned according to the character and personality of the God evoked.

However, this does not preclude us from changing their name and using it.

For instance, I know people who, in order to avoid persecution from their extremely Catholic families, saw the need to change the gods' names to Jesus and Mary, thereby preventing their relatives from persecuting them. And they could even pray in unison, despite the fact that they were praying to different gods. Along with common names, there are "secret" god names that are used by the coven within the circle and are only revealed to the initiated.

By examining the Sabbats, we can see how the facets of these gods exercise control over each season of the year and why.

THE EXISTENCE MANAGEMENT PLAN

The existence of alternate worlds or dimensions is a central tenet of numerous secret traditions. Wicca has been influenced by a variety of Eastern philosophies on this subject, but has retained the Old Religion's pre-Christian concepts. All things originate on three planes, as depicted in ancient Greek texts and then in Celtic tradition. They continue to be a part of a number of Wiccan traditions. Other Wiccan groups have fully embraced the Seven Planes of Existence, which are prevalent in Oriental concepts and contradict the Three Planes principle. Additionally, there are groups that incorporate Western Occultism into Wicca. We will examine the concept of these plans from the perspective of Modern Wicca.

THE ASTRAL ELEVENTH ELEVENTH ELEVENTH

The Astral Plane is an integral part of the Wicca Mysteries.

This is a difficult dimension to define because it is compressed into numerous realities and comparisons.

It is possible to say that space and time are inextricably linked. It is also a state of consciousness related to imagination, but more specifically within the kingdom governed by mental images, as opposed to the kingdom governed by simple thoughts or sounding awake. The Astral Plane is the Plane of Force, whereas the Physical Plane is the Plane of Form.

The dream world is one of the gateways to the Astral World. The initiate is instructed in the mysteries' teachings on how to control his dreams. Once the Dream has been programmed and prepared, it can be conducted and directed, and then the portal to the astral world is opened, allowing the initiate to enter and exit freely. Certain initiates prefer to establish a temple in the dream world, from which they can transmit influences to the Astral realm without physically entering it.

The Astral world's matter is referred to as Astral Light. It, like clay, can be modelled and moulded using the energy of our emotions and feelings. We create beings known as "Way of Thought" (thought-forms) in this etheric substance to act as conduits for greater forces. This matter is influenced not only by physical dimension emanations but also by those from Higher Dimensions, such as the Divine and Spiritual kingdoms. Thus, superior plans generate events and situations in the astral plane that manifest in the physical plane (unless that other energy modifies them in some way). This is where the Art of Divination enters the picture. It is built on the foundation of metaphysical science. If a person can discern what is manifesting on the physical plane through the images they are forming on the astral plane, they can discern what is manifesting on the physical plane.

However, we must understand that divination is the art of foreseeing future events. The constant flow of emotions passing through the astral dimension can alter the Astral images that encourage or give life to that event.

Thus, in Divination, we see what will occur if the patterns remain unchanged. Nothing is fixed in time in the Hidden Teachings; nothing will happen in our lives even if we do not want it to (except the death of the physical body). The major events of our lives, on the other hand, are imprinted on our spirits when our souls are born into a physical body.

This is the metaphysical underpinning of Astrology, alternatively known as Astral or Stellar Impression. Our natal (or astral) chart reveals the major patterns that have been drawn for us in each physical life, as well as our spiritual strength and weakness. We have the ability to work and change them because we possess free will.

THE PRINCIPLES OF THE ELEMENTARY PLANE

The Elemental Plane, or Plane of the Forces, is also included in the Teachings of the Mysteries, or Occult Teachings. This plane embodies the actions of the four creative forces or elements, which are responsible for everything that manifests and shapes in the physical dimension.

By examining these elements and the process by which they manifest, the fifth element known as Spirit becomes apparent.

This element is superior to the other four. If the four Elements represent the circle's points, the fifth is the circle itself!

The earth element is solid and embodies the metaphysical concept of the Law. Air is the Intellect's element and embodies the Metaphysical concept of Life. Fire is an active element that embodies the metaphysical concept of Light. Water is a fertile element that embodies the metaphysical concept of love. The Elemental Plane's various aspects are entwined with everything a Wiccan does or experiments with in their lives. They are encased in magic through spells, invocations, the consecration of amulets, tools, and the circle itself. They metaphysically reflect the Wiccan's psyche and emotions.

The individual's personality and any emotional instability are directly proportional to the balance of the elements that make up that person. Manna, numen, or more commonly referred to as elementals, is the awareness of these elements. The earth elementals are spirits whose vibration is so close to that of the Earth that they can alter its mineral composition and also exert influence over rocks, flora, and fauna. The elementals of the air are spirits whose vibration is inextricably linked to the energy emitted by all living things' electro impulses. Additionally, they have control over the mind and nervous system.

The elementals of fire are spirits whose vibrational frequencies are extremely similar to those of emotional energies such as joy, love, hate, fear, and other strong emotions. Additionally, they control emotions and the overall state of the body's metabolism. Water elementals are spirits whose vibrations are similar to those of fluids. They exert control over the balance of moisture and fluids in the environment, as well as the rest of nature.

The presence of these elements animates and influences all creation (or the lack thereof). Each object that is manifested possesses both a material and a spiritual nature. It is shaped by material nature and given life by spiritual nature. Everything physical, however, has a spiritual counterpart. The Zodiac contains the metaphysical correspondences of the elements, which aid in the preparation of the astral chart. Empedocles, a Pythagoras student, was the first to introduce the Four Elements doctrine and incorporate it into Astrology. Around 475 BC, he taught in his homeland of Sicily, presenting the four elements as the quadruple root of all things. This is the traditional image derived from his teachings in European occultism:

Taurus, Virgo, and Capricorn are earth signs. Gemini, Libra, and Aquarius are air signs.

Aries, Leo, and Sagittarius have a combination of hot and wet fire.

Extremely hot and arid Cancer, Scorpio, and Pisces are water signs. They are cold and wet. SUMMERTIME (Summer Country) Summerland is a term commonly used by Wiccans to refer to the other World or Beyond to which the souls of the deceased travel at the conclusion of their physical lives. It could be considered a kind of paradise, comparable to some indigenous traditions' Land of Happy Hunting.

Summerland exists on the astral plane and is experienced uniquely by each individual, depending on the spiritual vibrations he brings to that plane of existence. How long does one remain there? It is contingent upon each individual's capacity to release and resolve the burdens carried from life to life, which cause them to be the object of reincarnation in the physical plane. Each individual's existence in the Summerland provides an opportunity to learn and comprehend the lessons of previous lives and how they relate to previous lives experienced by that soul.

It is referred to as "time of rest and recovery" in Wiccan theology. After that time period has passed, the Elemental Plane begins to stretch the individual toward reincarnation in whatever dimension is compatible with the individual's spiritual condition.

The soul's reincarnation is determined by the plane of forces and can be poured into the vortex of a sexual union occurring on the Physical Plane. According to hidden teachings, the soul is poured into the physical plane that best prepares you for the lessons you must learn along the path of evolution in order to complete the reincarnation cycle. A loss of pregnancy, according to the Hidden Teachings, indicates that the creature's soul is no longer required to return to the physical world, but that he only required a brief appearance in physics matter to balance the etheric elementary properties required for its spiritual body.

The other reason this occurred is that the parents required that lesson in order to evolve spiritually, creating a soul that was not reincarnated or required physical existence. Not only in this area, but also in others, this soul is referred to as the teachings of the incarnation of higher spirits such as Buddha or Jesus.

THE SUSPICIOUS DIMENSIONS

According to hidden philosophies, creation is divided into four kingdoms: Spiritual, Mental, Astral, and Physical. For the purposes of this book, we will analyse only the interior dimensions, as these are integral to the Mysteries' internal mechanism. There are physical and spiritual planes of existence, just as there are physical planes of existence. Each plane is believed to be a reflection of the upper plane. This concept is the source of the occult expression "How is it top down?"

Every immediate inferior plane essentially manifests the "Thought Form" generated in the immediate superior plane. In magic, the practitioner establishes his desire on a higher plane in order for it to manifest on the lower plane. The following are the seven planes.

1- The Final Dimension

2- Dimension of the Divine

3- Dimensions of the Spiritual

4- Aspect of the mind

5- Dimension of the Astral

6- Dimension of the Elemental (Plan of the Forces)

7- Dimensions Physical (Plane of Forms)

The elementary plane is located directly on the plane of forms. Everything that occurs on the physical plane is inextricably linked to it.

Dimensions behave similarly to a row of domino pieces; one pushes against the next, and the chain begins. This is a physical law, as well as a metaphysical one (as above is below), and it explains how magic spells work. This law governs the internal mechanism of the planes. Each plane vibrates in response to the vibrations transmitted by another plane.

Above the plane of forces is the Astral plane, an ethereal realm that contains the collective consciousness's "forms of thought." It is here that the heavens and hells of Religious beliefs exist, fueled by the physical plane's thoughts and Religious emotions. On this plane, we can manifest our desires and fears. From the moment we are born, each of us possesses a portion of the creative spark that created us. We can also make use of that same force.

Our imaginative minds operate in this manner. The consciousness that created us functions normally; the only difference is that we are a spark rather than the source. The creative process is virtually identical in all ways to the one we use to create magic. For instance, suppose I decide to construct a pulpit capable of holding papers during a speech. To begin, I must visualise it in my mind. That thought will traverse the seven planes' various states. The divine plane will be infused with the Latest plane's spark. The spiritual plane will envision the plane, the mental plane will visualise it, the astral plane will manifest it in etheric matter, the elementary plane will contribute the way of thinking, and the physical plane will contribute the substance... and abracadabra... we have the pulpit!!!

In simple terms, the need above prompts me to consider how I might satisfy that need. I eventually form an idea and then refine it until I can visualise it in my mind. Once I have a clear mental image of it, I draw it on paper. Then I gather the necessary construction materials and begin assembling it. Once I've completed the assembly, I'll have the desired object and my work will be complete.

Magic is a creative art form. We work with the Astral substance. We have the ability to create with our thoughts because of the creative Spark. We create in accordance with the divine blueprint for the planes. Major is the emotion, more precisely the thought, and thus the Astral Plane's corresponding response. To effect changes in the physical world (magically), we must first effect changes in the astral plane. The magic ritual's purpose is to elevate and direct the energy (which contains the form of thought) to the Astral Plane. The ritual's symbols, gestures, colours, and elements are all forms of astral communication. Additionally, they generate the necessary images to unite all participants and form a collective conscience.

Each contributes a unique set of vibrations to the magical ritual. The modes of thought begin to manifest in the astral plane, where they serve as conduits for superior forces. The ritual energises those forms; as a result, the channels open and the forces gain strength.

Then, depending on the nature of the work, the raised energy will ascend to the Astral Plane or descend from the divine plane (as in the case of divine invocation rituals).

THE CODE OF THE WICCA

The name WICCA is derived from the contraction of the English term WITCHCRAFT and is derived from the celtic word WICCA. This refers to female priestesses, who will be dubbed witches. Wicca religion is the name given to the mother of all magic, who bases her beliefs on natural forces: the wiccan motto or Wicca religion's governing principle simply states: "feel free to share the arts of magic, develop and use your being to be psychic, and do whatever you want, as long as the outcome does not cause harm to anyone."

WHAT IS PROHIBITED?

Before performing any ritual, initiates believe it is critical to keep the Wiccan motto in mind, especially those that may be considered unethical or manipulative in nature. They ensure that if you violate it, even unintentionally, an instant of negative karma is generated, which means you must exercise extreme caution and think twice before using magic or psychic powers to exact revenge on an adversary.

WHAT IS PERMITTED?

If you believe it is necessary, feel free to make changes or minor additions to any spell (herbs, oils, incense, etc.) as long as the magical properties remain the same; however, the moon phase during which the spell is to be performed must not be changed or the spell's results will be affected. Finally, after casting a spell, you should express gratitude to the Goddess for her presence and protection, followed by a de-meditation ritual to unwind.

WHAT IS SUGGESTED TO DO?

It is recommended to always resolve conflicts with positive magical energy and to avoid focusing on the negative. Additionally, the ancient sorceresses assert that if you intentionally harm or manipulate another person through magic or another form of evil, you will pay a penalty of triple the desired evil. Reason - whenever a helping spell is cast on another, positive karma is obtained as a result.

THE MAGICAL LAWS OF WICCAN

1. As long as you do not cause harm to anyone, you may do whatever you want.

2. If you are aware that the Rede is being violated, you must fight back vigorously.

3. In debates, look, listen, and maintain your judgement; allow your silence to be long, your thoughts to be clear, and your words to be well-chosen.

4. Never run over, threaten, or speak ill of anyone. 5. Always be true, and thus avoid great evils.

6. Never bargain for a lower price on your Tools.

7. Keep your body, your clothes, and your home clean. 8. Avoid taking on tasks that you will be unable to complete, and if you must, work diligently to complete them correctly and within the allotted time.

9. Honor, care for and heal the Earth

10. Use only what you require and return as much as possible to the Earth as an offering, thereby nourishing the cycle of life 11. Do not judge those who follow other paths, but offer them love and assistance.

12. Do not steal from humans, animals, or spirits; if you cannot meet your community's needs, return to it.

13. Extend hospitality and friendship to strangers who pay a visit.

14. Never join or marry someone you do not love. 15. Respect other people's unions and commitments, and avoid relationships with those who will cause harm to another person.

16. Raise your children with kindness; feed, clothe and bring them home whenever possible. Demonstrate your love and affection for them. Instill in them courage and wisdom.

17. You will not own slaves and will abstain from any organisation, state, or community that permits such practises.

18. Be fair and honest in all of your dealings with others, adhering to both the letter and spirit of each contract you enter into.

19. The High Priests will rule the Coven as the gods' representatives.

20. Once it is established that these individuals have sufficient rank, the High Regent Priests will choose who they will have per second.

21. Within the Circle, the High Priests' commands and wishes are law.

22. The High Priests exercise authority in their capacities as Magicians, Counselors, and Fathers.

23. If there is a disagreement between you, let the High Priests summon the elders, who will render a judgement after hearing both sides together and separately.

24. If the High Priests determine that it is necessary to punish, suspend, or expel any member, this must be done in private and accepted gracefully by the member. 25. He who does not wish to work under the High Priests will seek another Coven or will seek another if it possesses the necessary range. He and any members accompanying him should abstain from contact with the old Coven for a period of time until the Covens re-establish a harmonious relationship bond.

26. If a High Priest leaves the Coven and returns during his regency, he must be accepted as if nothing had happened. If you do not return, you must rename Sumo to the person who was supplying the retired person; unless there are valid reasons to do so.

27. After the Council-established period, High Priests must resign with grace to make way for new High Priests.

28. Any High Priest who consents to the Rede's violation must be expelled 29. Before the Coven performs the magic, a consensus must be reached to ensure that no one is harmed.

30. The circle must be conjured and cleansed properly. To enter the circle, the Wiccan must be prepared and purified.

31. Without the consent of the Coven Council, no one can tell outsiders when or where Coven will meet.

32. In Wicca, refrain from gossiping or speaking ill of anyone.

33. Never deceive the Elders or anyone associated with Wicca.

34. Only Wiccans will be able to see the hidden mysteries; however, with the consent of the council, family members or friends may witness the ceremony.

35. No one should reveal to outsiders what Wiccan is, or provide names or other information that could jeopardise the Arts, or bring them into conflict with local laws or those who persecute them.

36. Keep the teachings of your Coven, as well as your rituals and the things you learned, in your book of shadows.

37. No one may enter the circle with those with whom they are at odds. In a dispute, no one has the authority to invoke any other law than Wicca's or to invoke any other authority than the High Priests and the Elders.

38. It is acceptable to be compensated for work performed with your hands, but not for work performed within a circle. Never accept payment for the use of magic or for teachings in the circle's arts.

39. Never use magic to demonstrate your superiority.

40. Contribute your talents, work, and earnings to Coven and noble causes that honour the Gods. Recognize those who devote their time and energy to arts service without receiving anything in return.

41. Never do anything that would discredit the Gods or Wicca.

Purpose Statement

Our objectives are as follows:

1. Follow the Wiccan Network's guidelines for living in a way that honours the Gods.

2. Investigate and practise Wiccan beliefs and traditions, with a particular emphasis on the British Isles' traditions.

3. Encourage and support one another within Coven in terms of health, development, and aspirations

4. Perform Wiccan Rituals in conjunction with Sabbats, Esbats, and special events in order to observe the seasons, perform magic, recognise rites of passage, and honour the Gods.

5. Respect the Earth and all of its creatures as sacred; and work to heal and protect our community's environment.

6. Teach Wiccan beliefs and traditions to members and students, artists' siblings and sisters, and anyone else who is receptive to alternative spiritual paths.

7. Dedication

8. Each member of this Coven must be deeply committed to living their beliefs and fully commit themselves to achieving these goals through their activities and lives.

69

Membership Requirements

Individuals will be admitted to the Coven upon the recommendation of the High Priest or High Priestess, the Council's approval, and the consensus of the Initiates (members assets). No one can be denied membership on the basis of their gender, race, ethnic origin, sexual orientation, physical disability, or age (as long as they can demonstrate that they are adults).

Participation And Membership At Various Levels

The following individuals participate in the Coven's activities:

1. Guests: interested individuals who may participate in open activities or enter the Coven when accompanied by an initiate and with the consent of the remaining Initiates.

2. Congregants: individuals who identify as Wiccan and actively participate in and support the Coven's open activities.

3. Dedicators: individuals who have devoted themselves to the study of the Wicca path, with the approval of all active Initiates receiving arts instruction. Then, once the time for the initiation has been established, the individual may request it or withdraw from the Coven without incurring any obligations. Coven membership is reserved for the following individuals:

I - Initiates Individuals who have been active in Coven or on the Wicca path for a year and a day and have met all of the requirements of the Coven Council for initiation and have been initiated Priests of the gods.

II - Second Degree Initiates: Individuals who have been active in Coven or the walk (having attempted it) for two years and two days and have met the requirements for the Second Degree

Initiation as recommended by byte High Priests and approved by the Initiates' consensus.

III - Third Degree Initiates: Individuals who have attained the Second Degree and have demonstrated proficiency in ritual creation, leadership, teaching, counselling group processes, and administration; and who have been recommended by the High Priests and approved by the Initiates' consensus. Additional titles of recognition: Teachers of the Arts titles will be awarded to those who achieve specific accomplishments. First Grade initiates who have demonstrated proficiency in specific disciplines and have been approved and tested by the Second and Third Degree initiates will receive the title of Teacher in the Arts, which may include the following:

1. Tarot, Astrology, I Chin, Runes, Lithomancy, Radio esthesia, Dream Interpretation

2. Herbalism: amulets, incenses, oils, and health products, among others.

3. Healing Arts: Naturopathy, aromatherapy, psychic healing, crystal healing, Reiki, or other healing arts

4. Arts involving Relatives: Animal magic, Totems, and morphing forms, for example.

5. Talismans: talismans and amulets are created.

6. Ritual Instruments: creation of ritual instruments

7. Psychic Arts: astral projection, telepathy, clairvoyance, and psychometrics, among others.

8. Enchantment: Spells, Charms, Songs, and Mantras

9. Enthusiasm: Trancework, Meditation, Hypnosis, Pathworking

10. Music: Music, storytelling, and theatre, among other things.

Additional titles may be created in response to Coven's requirements and with the advice's approval.

Membership Status Any person's membership may be withdrawn, suspended, or terminated at the discretion of the Coven Council for a lack of assistance, participation, or for violating the Wiccan Administration network and operations.

The Council of the Coven

They have the final say in how Coven is administered. Membership: The council is comprised of all initiates. Dedicators may be invited to meetings.

Scope: The Council deliberates on and resolves issues pertaining to the following: activity programme, dedication, initiating, and finance. Memberships and financial resources. Community outreach: In the advice, the High Priest or High Priestess sits in the presidency chair. When he is present, he immediately assumes that position in the hierarchical rank.

Consensus will be used to make decisions. If the Initiates are unable to agree, the final decision will be made by the Regent, who will consider what has been discussed and make a decision. Unless the Regent is the High Priest or High Priestess, all decisions must be made during the same board meeting.

The Council must meet at least once every three months, or as required by an initiate. Quorum must consist of at least three-quarters of the Coven's Active initiates. Crafts and Employment High Priests (3rd Grade): President of the Coven Council, Coordination of the Study Program, Counseling, Ritual Leadership,

Supervision of other officers, Initiation Direction, Supervision of the work of second and third degree candidates. Coven representative, Maintaining harmony within the Coven, providing guidance on tithing the Coven's works, defending the Coven when threatened, and serving as the Final Authority on Ritual, Initiation, Ordination, and everything else related to religion.

Maiden (2nd Grade): Assists the High Priestess in her duties and fills in for him when he is unavailable. Sumoner (2nd Grade): Assists the High Priest in his duties and fills in for him when he is unavailable.

Notify Coven members of meetings and other significant events. Watchtower: Responsible for Coven Security, as well as ritual and special activity planning.

Maintains minutes of Coven Council meetings and Coven property reports. Additional functions can be created on a temporary or permanent basis to meet the needs of Coven. All Dedicators and Members must conduct themselves according to the Wiccan Network's guidelines, the Law of Return, Wiccan Laws, and the Gods within.

Esbats are typically held on nights of the full or new moon. Sabbats will be held on the corresponding day or on a weekend closer to the date, with the exception of Samhain, which will be held on October 31st. Once the dates for the rituals are set, they cannot be changed unless more than two members are unable to attend, at which point a new date will be set by consensus of all Initiates.

The Coven Council may determine as many presentation seminars and open classes as necessary. Dedicator and Initiate classes must be taught at least once a month on a date determined by the Coven Council. The Coven Council must establish the curriculum. No fee will be charged for the dictated classes that are required as part of the Coven curriculum.

The New Moons are exclusive esbats reserved for devout devotees and initiates.

Full Moons are open to anyone who wishes to attend. Sabbats may be opened, but the Council must designate another date for Coven members to celebrate. Classes will be open or closed at the discretion of the Coven Council or High Priests. Dedicators and Initiates are required to attend all Rituals and Classes appropriate to their level.

First Grade Dedicators and Initiates are required to attend at least 75% of these activities; if this requirement is not met, your membership will be reviewed by the advisory. Second and Third Degree Initiates are exempt from this requirement, given the level of work expected of them at Coven. Coven tickets are funded through donations or revenue generated by community-based activities.

The Scribe is responsible for maintaining Coven's books and compiling reports for each meeting of the advice. Members' addresses, phone numbers, and any other information pertaining to specific members of Coven should be kept private and not revealed in front of non-members without the permission of the same.

Failure to respect a member's privacy is a serious offence that will result in his membership being terminated, as it is considered a breach of the Wiccan network. By consensus of the Coven Council, any part of these laws may be amended or changed.

THE SABBATS OF WICCA

The wiccan year is divided into eight Sabbats. These are days to rejoice with the gods and have fun. No magic is performed during the Sabbats unless it is absolutely necessary for health. However, joy and celebration abound.

Throughout history, prior to the persecutions, numerous covens gathered to celebrate. The number of sorcerers grew to several hundreds, all drawn from the region's covens.

CHAPTER 2:

CELEBRATE THE NUMBER OF WITCHCRAFT

The people congregate on a wooded hill along the Missouri River's shores. Around the full moon, stars twinkle above the surrounding trees. Between the ancient oaks, fireflies buzz, their lights flashing mysteriously. The air is still, still at night. Forty people encircle a blazing bonfire, their hands extended and their gaze drawn to a woman standing before the bonfire. An invocation to the Goddess arises from her silhouetted silhouette against the glow of their das.

The words, soft at first but growing in strength as they progress, flow freely from your mouth. "Moon goddess," she says, "every year on a full moon, we gather here in your honour." In the fire, sticks crackle. "Sun God, O Magnificent, all-powerful..." The invocation concludes. As the group begins to move slowly toward time, the woman raises her arms to the heavens. The people - some wearing hoods, others in more mundane attire - took their steps. They sing in a slow single tone, an incomprehensible principle. The wood squeaks. Moonlight seeps out.

Tap the floor with your bare feet. Fast. As they refocus their minds on their mission, the group practically flies around the go, and the woman standing in their way. After an indeterminate amount of time, the lonely woman simply stops them. The group immediately comes to a halt, and their members simultaneously point their hands at the figure. It shines, radiates, shakes, and directs energy to the Goddess, who is symbolised by the glowing sphere in heaven. Exhausted, the group sits on the bare earth, conversing and laughing as they share wine and crescent-shaped cakes. Your rite is complete. Popular magic is a subset of what is colloquially referred to as the sea of witchcraft.

The other half is represented by the Wiccan religion. Wicca is distinguished from other religions by at least five major characteristics: Goddess and God worship; reverence for the earth; acceptance of magic; acceptance of reincarnation; and absence of proselytism. Wiccans venerate both Goddess and God. According to Wiccans, Western religion's current dental care system is unbalanced. Waistband—it is referred to as the Godhead Deity (rather than the Goddess). The term "God the Father" is frequently used. Both the concept of "saviours" and its culmination, direct descendants of the male Deities, are found outside of Christianity. These organisations' representatives - officers, priests, and I - do more harm than good. They oppose tree-cutting strips that cover acres of land with concrete and tar. Because Wiccans regard the earth as a manifestation of the Goddess and God, they are concerned with their well-being: they lend the earth human energy in order to help her recover from the damage inflicted by humanity. As a result, Wicca is truly an Earth religion.

As previously stated, magic plays a role in almost all religions. She plays a more prominent role in Wicca than you do. Despite its popularity, Wicca is not religious magic. Without a doubt, practise is painful. Neither is religion magical. It is a religion that embraces magic, viewing it as a way to connect with divine, earthly, and human energies. Due to the fact that Wicca is a true religion, magic plays a minor role in their rituals. Even in a practical rite with a specific magical goal in mind, the Goddess and God are always invoked prior to sending the energy. The magical aspects of Wicca perplex the laity, perhaps because, in the majority of other religions, only priests or saviours are believed to be capable of channelling divine energy in a single mine. Wicca is not so exclusive; she regards magic as an inherent component of life and religion. Reincarnation is an ancient teaching that the majority of people believe in. It is regarded as reality in the Wiccan tradition. In its simplest form, riper-Carnation is a doctrine of rebirth - the phenomenon of incarnation in human form aimed at soul evolution regardless of gender or age. While reincarnation is not an external concept in any religion, including Wicca, she is happily accepted by the majority of Wiccans for providing answers to numerous everyday life questions and for explaining more mystical phenomena such as death, birth, and karma. "Reincarnation? Bah!" some may exclaim. That is exclusively an Eastern phenomenon. " Without a doubt, more information about their incarnation is available through the teachings of the region that is now known as India. However, the concept is as ancient as humanity itself. A seed is deposited in the soil. It sprouts and grows. They erupt. The sprouts continue to grow in length and flower. The seeds are deposited in the soil. The plant withers and withers, but a new plant will emerge from the soil the following spring. The doctrine of reincarnation may have evolved out of the need to conserve natural processes such as this one. Those who accept its reality, including a large number of Wiccans, found it reassuring.

The fifth most significant distinction between Wicca and the majority of other religions is the lack of proselytising. Nobody went; yahoo will be compelled to convert to Wicca. There are no threats of eternal fire and damnation, nor are there any penalties for not practising Wicca. Goddess and God are not jealous Deities, and Wiccans do not fear them or feel threatened by them. Candidates for initiation (which we will discuss in greater detail later in this book) do not condemn their previous faiths. Wicca is not a religion; it is a brainwashing and mind-control cult disguised as one.

Wiccans do not recruit new followers while harelipsing and rubbing their hands as new members join their religion. There are no Wiccan missionaries, "witnesses," or pressure groups. It may come as a surprise to those educated in the mentality of orthodox religions, but Wicca is founded on a secure and solid concept that is the polar opposite of the teachings of the majority of other religions: no religion is perfect for everyone. Perhaps it is not an exaggeration to assert that the greatest form of human vanity is to believe that their religion is the only Deity and that everyone will judge it as highly recommended by thinkers like you, while those who hold contrary beliefs are deceived, deluded, or ignorant. It's understandable that many religions and their adherents believe this and actively participate in conversion. Observing others convert to their restored faith reaffirms the converter's faith's genuineness. While some adherents of orthodox religions genuinely care about the souls of unbelievers, this concern is based on their religions' dull teachings. Politics is another facet of proselytising. If Religion A converts Country B, it gains political and economic influence in that country. The same is true for individuals. Orthodox religions wield unbridled political and financial influence. Political candidates backed by the major religions are continually elected to propose or support legislation that advances the religion's interests. This is all possible. To undercut (voters may disregard the true nature or extent of the applicant's ties to

79

organised religion), but the effect is identical. Money is also a strong motivator for spreading the word.

Today, religions established in the United States generate billions of dollars in monthly tax revenue. True, some of this money is donated to charity, but the majority of it goes to the religion's bureaucracy, fattening the bank accounts of those who control it. As a result, the more followers you have, the more money you earn. Wicca, on the other hand, is not like that. It is disorganised at the moment. There are national groups, but the majority of you are there for social and occasionally legal reasons. Regional Conferences

While Wiccans can attract hundreds of people, most local groups have fewer than ten members, and many Wiccans practise their religion independently. According to some, Wicca is not a financial institution and has no intention of becoming one. Students are not charged for initiating. Small fees, if any, are similar to those charged by various groups to cover food and beverage expenses. It is untrue to speak of a global organisation seeking to control the world. As are the fabrications about Wiccans attempting to coerce others into following their religion. They are simply not as insecure. Not to worry, the Wiccans are not out and about attempting to coerce young Jimmy into joining a convenor or convincing Aunt Sara to give up her savings. They are content with their religion being practised in their own unique way - whether alone or in community. There are distinctions between Wicca and other religions, as well as an overarching goal shared by all: union with the Divine.

Although it was written for solitary practitioners, the majority of it was written for group work, even if only one individual is involved in the circle's formation. It never hurts to emphasise that the aforementioned "Stone Spirits" are not disembodied human souls; they are not spirits, demons, or capitals. They are frequently

80

referred to as "Lord of the Tor-Watchers" or "Queens and Kings of the Elements" in some Wiccan traditions. These are elemental energies who have been invited to assist with the protection and to share your unique energy philosophy. This is a nearly universal practise in Wicca. The circle, in Wiccano's view, is the holiest place for honouring the Goddess and God, but it also serves another purpose: it contains and concentrates magical energy. This is a non-essential function. Certainly, the circle is not required for effective group or solitary magic practise.

The magic circle is essentially a non-physical, but real, temple in which humans - Wiccans - walk alongside Goddess and God. As such, it is a central feature of Wicca practise, but it is not required for group worship.

Wiccans can perform simple rituals alone on hills or while sitting on the beach and watching the water. As the sun rises or the moon sets, they can commune with the Goddess and God. A Wiccan group may decide to perform a ritual during a picnic or a stroll inland. They can simply sit or stand in a circle and practise your work without instruments. During all rituals other than spontaneous ones, however, the magic circle is typically constructed, and it is within it that the rites of worship and magic are performed. Wicca's temple is a circle (sphere) of energy.

CHAPTER 3:

MAGIC CIRCLE IS USUAL

There are numerous types of magic, and folk magic is merely one of them. The two other major categories - ceremonial and religious - do not fit our definition of Witchcraft because they are frequently lumped in with all other hidden practises under this umbrella term. However, a brief discussion of these two categories can help clear up some misunderstandings.

Magical Ceremonies

Ceremonial (or ritual) magic is a modern system founded on ancient and recent traditions. It is based on Sumerian, Egyptian, Indian, and Semitic magic, and has been influenced by Arab and later So thought. Freemasonry, as well as the secret societies that were popular in the 18th and 19th centuries in Britain and throughout Europe, also contributed to its current structure. Contrary to popular belief, wizard's ceremonials have nothing to do with the destruction or theft of monstrous spirits with fly heads' magic rings. They do not possess magical rugs or live in caves, and most emphatically do not suffocate victims with swords. They even do not use goblins as currency. Above all, they bear no resemblance to Witchcraft, except in the minds of the laity.

Ceremonial magicians' ritual structures, terminology, and objectives are frequently - but not always - aligned with the divine, with perfection and expansion of consciousness. Alternatively, as is frequently stated, "science and a conversation with a wizard's guardian angel." Isn't that a lofty spiritual objective? And highlights one of the fundamental distinctions between ceremonial magic and pop-up homes. Unlike the latter, ritual mages are typically unconcerned with the popular wizard's goals of love, healing, money, happiness, and protection. When such goals are attained through ceremonial magic (as in the creation of a talisman), it is frequently used as a means to an end - to accomplish the above union. For their part, wizards use rituals to resolve personal conflicts, while those with a rare mind seek something greater. Certain ceremonial wizards form groups known as stores or orders (such as the famous Golden Dawn - Golden Dawn, no. of T.) and incorporate elements of Egyptian religion into their magical works. Numerous rituals used by a small group of this magic shop in the late nineteenth century were published in Israel Regardie's The Golden Dawn, one of the most influential ma-already edited. Other wizards are attuned to more traditional religions. xas. The Middle Ages and Renaissance magical books included invocations to Jehovah, Adonai, and God and made extensive use of Judeo-Christian terminology. This is not heresy or farce, but an interpretation of the Christian myth in a different light. Naturally, this is not folk magic, in which power is transmitted without invoking a Deity. Ceremonial wizards are frequently quite unique.

Many practitioners practise their art alone, devoting lengthy evenings to reading ancient scriptures, preparing their "instruments of art," and studying Latin and Greek in order to perform their rituals more effectively. They read Aleister Crowley's works as well as those of William Gray, John Dee, Franz Bardon, Agrippa, and Dion Fortune, among others. Some devote their studies to alchemy, geomancy, Enochian magic, and other subjects as primary or secondary subjects. Ceremonial wizards are merely human beings who not only work with energy (that is, they practise ma-) but also seek something greater than the orthodox religions have to offer. They come with a long and colourful history, replete with fantastic events and exotic rituals and rites. They are not, however, Wizards.

Herbs

Perhaps the eivas were first used in magic and religion before being thrown into pans for culinary or medicinal purposes. At the moment, these aromatic treasures are being rediscovered by new generations of powerful wizards, who are busy harvesting, mixing, cooking, and preparing these aromatic treasures. Herbs, like crystals, contain extremely potent and distinct energies that are used in magic. Rose petals can be scattered throughout the house to promote peace. They can also be placed between pink candles to bring love into the popular wizard's life. CA-it can be burned to stimulate intelligence; lavender flowers can be added to baths as purifiers; and sandalwood can be burned to raise the ion and facilitate mediumistic experiences. In folk magic, an incredible variety of herbs - including fruits, trees, flowers, roots, chestnuts, seeds, algae, ferns, and grass - are used. This is a form of magic that we have not forgotten entirely, dear people, as we continue to offer flowers, use perfumes and essences of vegetables to attract mates, and serve meals enhanced with herbs to potential lovers (or we received them). Eivas can be burned as incense to release energies into the air, or they can be carried in their pockets and sprinkled throughout the house for a variety of magical purposes. Oils, essential oils, and magical concoctions are rubbed into the body or candles, added to baths, or used to anoint crystals and other ritual objects. Previously the domain of every healer and wizard, herbs are being reintroduced as instruments of power by a number of popular mages.

CHAPTER 4:

WICCA TERMINOLOGIES

This chapter is intended to be a concise overview of the most frequently used terms by sorcerers and witches, to serve as an introduction to the subject and then to allow for the analysis of more advanced topics:

BRUJERIA: is the use of magical techniques to manipulate nature; it operates on symbolic principles, is more or less explicit, violent, and bloody, and seeks not only benefit but also evil in exchange for monetary compensation. Although religion and high magic denigrate witchcraft, there are numerous macho prejudices against women who come from the church, and witchcraft was in many cases a spiritual technique that sought to unite the soul with nature through the forces of the elements; this aspect is being resurrected by wiccans.

FACING: is the practise of using magic to obtain benefits, and satisfying the ego entails the use of intelligence to sway cosmic laws in our favour. Although they are not as bloodthirsty and violent as witchcraft, they imply a poisoning of the soul and a mind that twists and becomes cynical. They employ the same laws of magic as witchcraft but are governed by the ego. Thus, sorcerers are referred to as black magicians.

WICCA is an ancient and Nordic term; it is the source of the term Withcraft.

Nowadays, Wicca is a cultural movement dedicated to redressing historical injustices against witches and reclaiming their rituals from a spiritual perspective, as a union of the soul with nature. Hopefully, witchcraft will no longer be perceived as wrong and will be understood by the globalised culture, because wicca combats its own negative aspects and celebrates and invokes the positive natural forces in the experience of soul self-discovery.

MAGIC: It is the art and practise of manipulating nature and its forces in order to effect change. It is typically classified into various types of magic, with its two primary branches being Goercia and Teurgia. Natural magic, which is performed with potions and objects, vocal magic, gestural magic, which employs magnetic passes, and etheric energy and thought-based magic, which are the most powerful.

GOERCIA: This is the name given to the magic used on demons and inferior spirits.

This is the traditional method taught in magical manuals and grimoires such as Little Alberto, the Book of Almaziel, and the salomonicos.

THEURGY: is the branch of magic that is applied to the spiritual, to the bright forces; it entails the invocation and work with angels and entities, mental magic, and karmic transmutation

87

processes; their rituals are drawn from the great religions and include divine and angelic invocations.

NIGROMANCE: the branch of magic and sorcery concerned with the evocation of the dead, obtaining clairvoyance or messages from the dead, as well as ceremonies of invocation of the dead and works of magic involving spirits and energies of already deceased people. Although it is the most despised aspect of magic, its effect on matter and nature is significant.

Today, few shamans practise it, and the most powerful necromancers are the Central American Vodu and Santero priests.

AQUELARRE: This is also referred to as sabbat (sabath). It is the meeting of the witches; it began with a narration of each witch's misdeeds, continued with a banquet (with either great delicacies or truculent characters, depending on the version), and concluded with a great orgie.

COVENS: It is said that covens were celebrated in Germany's Blockberg and Koterberg mountains, as well as the plain of Barabona in Soria (Spain). Much of what is said about covens are versions extracted through torture, much of what is said is symbolic and esoteric rather than literal, and much of what the witches claimed to do, such as flying on brooms and unions with beastly beings, were the result of hallucinogenic mixtures discovered and reproduced containing belladonna, poppy, mandragora, and other hallucinogenic products that produce the same type of hallucination. The majority of coven phenomena, visions, and rituals occur in the astral plane and are internal astral bass experiences in low and lugubrious regions.

GRIMORIO: Witches kept a journal in which they cast spells and observed their effects, ensuring that they were transmitted and endured. The most famous is the BOOK OF SHADOWS, which has been mocked by mediocre television series; however, the book exists and is a collection of basic and traditional rituals that spans several volumes; the most famous grimoires are mentioned in the middle ages when the uglesia forbids books other than the bible, and grimoires become almost science books and instructional manuals. Additionally, the majority of grimoires contain recipes containing ingredients that are impossible to obtain and yield dubious results. They also exaggerate the magic of invocation of spirits and submit to the intake and proof of all Menjunjes and prepared class, but they all have a solid foundation of recipes, practises, and some rituals, as well as a great deal of mental preparation and suggestion to produce the desired effects on their surroundings, but some recipes actually work and are not just suggestions. The most famous grimoires are the various clavicles of Salomon, the book of Raziel, the books by John Dee with enoquiana magic (angelica), the agrippa treaties, the books of arbatel and Abremalin the magician, the grimoireslate as the little and great alberto, the book of cipriano, pactum, and several hundred more, some of greater value than others. They are difficult to obtain and require extensive study, as their recipes frequently conceal esoteric and symbolic descriptions beneath the surface of real or physical processes.

CONJURO: Spells were formulas with words that combined ancient languages and strange rhymes, and they were essentially a vibratory projection through which desire manifested itself through the word and created a projection in the etheric planes that then rushed and manifested on the physical plane over others. Because spells are complicated and already contain formulas for the evocation of entities, grimoires typically contain some magical recipes as well as additional spells or disguised children.

FACT: It is a form of appearance manipulation based on the manipulation of ether fluids flowing through the etheric body and aura. The spells altered the appearance of objects or people,

89

manipulated etheric energy or astral substance, and are already considered to be typical magical operations.

CHARMING: it is a spell that is cast on a location, parapsychology refers to this as an infestation, when a location appears to accumulate and manifest conflicting and phenomenal energies, referred to as poltergeist by science today, enchantment is a mantle of generally oppressive energy that is projected and confined to a location, and that energy encloses and affects entities present there, having these that manifest the enchantments are similar to the e

FILTER: preparations made up of liquids that also involve the manipulation of subtle fluids in order to impress and affect people's minds and emotions are classic filters used to divert enemies, induce love, and manipulate psychologically through witchcraft rituals. In general, the filter can be beneficial up to the point where it becomes harmful and a tool for evil, which is usually detrimental to the subject who ends up losing or ruining what the filter was intended to accomplish.

Because the filter is essentially an illusion that can be exploited as an opportunity, its duration is brief and is frequently ruined and decomposed in this manner.

EIGHTH OR POTION: prepared primarily from liquids, which included drugs and substances that exhibited the analogical properties or correspondences ascribed by thematic to objects, minerals, vegetables, animals, and emotional forces that related to and reflected the planetary and angelic forces, which in turn reflected the cosmic and divine attributes.

MEJUNJE OR MENJUNGE: narcotic herb preparation that gave witches the sensation of flight; by extension, any herbal preparation that has an effect on nature, such as extraordinary cures, divination, or the discharge of negative energies.

90

INCUBO: the devil disguised as a man, which is why women used to present themselves to seduce him and convert him to a witch.

SUCUBO: the devil disguised as a woman; his malefic function was to seduce men; the majority of primitive saints were tempted by sucubos.

ENGENDROS: The beings produced by the union of humans and diabolic beings as sucubos and incubations, contrary to popular belief, there are several chronicles of the births of these fantastic beings, who manifested an odd appearance and were surrounded by even stranger phenomena.

HOMUNCLE, HOMOID, OR ANDROID: a creature created artificially; in the cabin is the clay golem; in voodoo are the resurrected zombies; homunculi are creatures created in alchemists' laboratories, giving rise to legends such as Frankenstein's; androids are creatures animated through magical or mechanical processes; celebrate the android that destroyed the shots of Aquino, the homunculus of Paracels, some creatures that

DAIMON: According to Greek tradition and as cited by Plato and Pythagoras, it is confused with other beliefs such as the holy guardian angel and the djinns or Persian geniuses, despite the fact that it appears to be a metaphor for consciousness and its mysterious voice.

METAMORPHOSIS: the belief that concoctions and special rites can transform humans into animals (preferably wolves). In general, the transformation is associated with the moon, as it represents the repressed subconscious forces that manifest themselves at night; thus, the transformation is an expression of the aura or ethereal body that possesses an animistic trait. While the transformation into wolves or vampires is the most common, witches have been said to be transformed into cats or toads. As for the transformation itself, it appears to be a transformation of the ethereal body, the aura, which manifests as the features. This process has been documented in mediums that have materialised ectoplasm, which is an ethereal substance materialised, and the process would be similar.

BLACK MASS: a parody of the Christian mass performed by the devil in covens, concluding with a blasphemous kiss on the buttocks of the officiants. Although the origins of the Catholic mass are unknown, the ritual elements of the Catholic mass are Babylonian, whereas the Mass Black is a celebration of nature and the inferior and powerful aspects of instinct.

DEMONIC: the demonic is a descent to the base, to instinct and power, to violence and chaos, just as meditation is an ascent to the regions of light or knowledge.

CONCLUSION

We appreciate your perseverance in completing Wicca. For Beginners, we hope this article was informative and equipped you with the necessary tools to accomplish your goals, whatever they may be.

The time has come to cast aside our preconceived notions and examine Witchcraft's stated goals: spiritual conquest, happiness, and financial security. Where is the heinousness in this? Where are the atrocities perpetrated by zillions of sermons and that continue to contribute to religious crimes today?

Horror exists solely in the minds of those who are ignorant of the truth, and this ignorance breeds fear. This fear is stoked by representatives of other religions seeking to increase their adherents.

Wicca and popular magic are gentle and loving and are practised by hundreds of thousands of people. That is the reality of Witchcraft in the modern era.

www.ingramcontent.com/pod-product-compliance
Lightning Source LLC
LaVergne TN
LVHW020926200726
843506LV00011B/1832